DUCKING
& DIVING

BRITAIN, BASKETBALL AND BRUNEL IN THE 1980S

DUCKING & DIVING

BRITAIN, BASKETBALL AND BRUNEL IN THE 1980S

DB
PUBLISHING

To Carol, the only person to suffer both the seven years covered in this book,
and the ten that it took to write it.

First published in Great Britain in 2012 by The Derby Books Publishing Company Limited, 3 The Parker
Centre, Derby, DE21 4SZ.

Copyright © John Kirkland, 2012

ISBN 978-1-78091-051-2

Photos reproduced with the kind permission of the Uxbridge Gazette.

CONTENTS

FOREWORD

I take responsibility for this book, but there are many people without whom it would never have seen the light of day. They should assume a portion of the notoriety, too.

Thanks, in particular, to my Mum and late father, for their patience and support during my singularly unproductive life. I hope this book will explain how at least part of it has been spent, and that the results are not too disappointing. Also to staff at DP Publishing, for taking on such a quirky project, and their professionalism in bringing it to fruition, to Sally Preece, of Brunel Sports Centre, for providing many of the photographs, and to the Uxbridge Gazette for allowing us to reproduce some of theirs.

I would also like to remember the late Pete Jacques, occasional teacher and full-time basketball fanatic, whose trip from Edlington Comprehensive School provided my first basketball experience. Tragically, Pete did not survive to read this book. He would have found it more interesting than my history essays, although that is a pretty low threshold.

The real heroes of this story are the players, coaches, directors and supporters of the Brunel Ducks Basketball Club, whose contributions I appreciate even more now than three decades ago. Thanks for the memories, guys. I hope you regard those recorded here as happy ones, and that some, at least, are accurate. If not, please accept my apologies.

John Kirkland

PROLOGUE

This is an unfashionable book. It tells the story of an unfashionable team, who played an unfashionable sport, at an unfashionable university in an unfashionable suburb of London. It takes place in the 1980s, a decade so unfashionable that a generation of politicians and economists now disclaim any responsibility for it.

The book was conceived by two very unfashionable people. It was October 2001. Tim and I, only known supporters of Rotherham United Football Club to live in the London Borough of Harrow, were travelling home after a very unsatisfactory evening. Tim and I are self-confessed 'anoraks'. According to my dictionary, an anorak is 'a socially inadequate person with a hobby considered to be boring'. And, usually, I might add, one who pursues the said hobby in an obsessive amount of detail.

It had been a night for anoraks. We had been to see Rotherham play at Wimbledon before the lowest crowd ever for a match in the second tier of English football – officially reported as 849. Or rather I had. Tim had travelled to south London with the express purpose of standing *outside* the ground, along with home fans, boycotting the game in protest at the impending move of their club to a new venue some 50 miles away in Milton Keynes.

Tim and his conspirators had counted every single spectator going into the game. They aimed to prove that, even at 849, the club were over estimating their support. I had spent a large part of the second half counting the crowd also, but from inside the ground. It was a very boring game. We both reckoned that there were no more than 600 there. We speculated that the official figure probably included season ticket holders who had not turned up, media and, for all we knew, players.

I felt qualified to speculate on this topic. Falsifying crowd numbers was one of many misdemeanours of which had I been guilty some 20 years previously, as a director of a long forgotten semi-professional basketball club called the Brunel Ducks. The Ducks were long forgotten to most people, but not to Tim.

Tim had never been to Brunel University, or attended a basketball game. He did not even live in London at the time when this story begins, but *he* had heard of the Brunel Ducks. He knew, too, that here was a tale that needed telling, and advised that I should do just that. Tim promptly got off the train, disappeared to the pub for a last drink, and forgot his advice. For me, the damage was done.

Anoraks do not represent a mass market. One day, it will be fashionable to be unfashionable. Then thousands of people will read this book, first editions will be worth a fortune and you will be glad that you bought, stole or were given this one. In the meantime, I predict that this story will interest about 20 people. Unless basketball has changed in the last two decades, most of these will expect their copies for free. All will read out of self-interest. A few will want to see whether there is any potential for making money from a libel action. Health and safety officials, tax inspectors and the management of Brunel University might want to check how many of their rules were broken. Officials of the English Basket Ball Association will want to see if any of theirs were actually observed.

The saving grace is that this story really happened. It is part of the history of British basketball, and Brunel University, whether they like it or not. It might also raise the odd smile for anyone who remembers the 1980s, or has ever supported any team, in any sport, against seemingly impossible odds. If no one else wants to tell it, then I will. Come to think of it, if anyone else does plan to tell it (and they are certainly taking their time to decide), then I'd better get my version in first.

For what follows is unashamedly my version. It draws on my memory and a ragged collection of souvenirs from my attic. If time, a tendency to dramatise, or to inflate my own role have exaggerated some details, then I am sorry. Any such deficiencies should not be allowed to detract from the basic tale, of how a random group of people set out from the Brunel University Sports Centre with no experience, few players and very little money, and returned to the same building one April evening less than seven years later clutching the National Basketball Championship Trophy.

That bit definitely happened. I have the score sheets to prove it, but doubt whether that will be necessary. Quite simply, the story that follows is one that you just couldn't make up.

GENESIS

It was lunchtime, on the first Thursday in June, 1980. I was walking across the small zebra crossing that bisected the Brunel University campus, outside the main administration building. Halfway across, a car screeched to a halt. Instead of apologising, the driver shouted that he'd like a word with me. Lesson number one about basketball – no one ever apologises for anything.

The driver was Salih Basaga, doctoral student of cybernetics, tall, dark, handsome and, most important of all, a leading light in the Brunel Ducks Basketball Club. He had recognised me as a leading light in the Students Union – he had voted for me in my recent election as vice-president. He had also noticed me as a spectator at several Ducks games in the previous season. He wondered if I could help.

In fact, I had only attended two Ducks games. I would like to think that my being noticed reflected my fame as a student politician. More likely, it reflected the lack of anyone else *to* notice. The average home attendance for the Brunel Ducks in 1979–80 was officially estimated at 93. From my recollection, this was a gross exaggeration. Perhaps, like the Wimbledon crowd over two decades later, it included the players and officials.

Salih's story was challenging, to say the least. He told how, throughout the 1970s, the Brunel basketball club had gradually incorporated players from outside the campus – some former students, some local residents. It had become one of the leading teams in Middlesex. When the second division of the National Basketball League had been established the previous year, it had seemed natural to try and take the club further.

Joining the national league had been a bigger step than anyone envisaged. In fact, Brunel was only allowed in by accident. The English Basket Ball Association, who managed the league, had never wanted them there. Ideally, they wanted to develop a national league based on large and instantly recognised cities. A club based on students – a transitory and intrinsically unreliable section of the population – did not exactly meet this profile. Nor did Uxbridge, an anonymous suburb of London best known for being at the end of the Metropolitan line, quite meet the criteria of being an instantly recognisable city. The application was rejected.

Events had then spun out of the English Basket Ball Association's control. By August, three of the teams so carefully selected for their reliability and permanence had folded. There was nothing else for it. If the authorities wanted a National League Second Division, they would have to all compromise their standards. They did so in a big way. Ten days before the start of the season, Brunel was asked to make the numbers up.

Everything about playing in the National League had been harder than expected. It had been difficult to expand the local league squad. The team started with a credible defeat at Brighton – they even led at half-time. By the time of their next league fixture, a full five weeks later, four of the squad, who between them had contributed 74 of the Ducks' 82 points in that first game, had left. The season had ended with just two wins from 14 games, and the team firmly anchored at the bottom of the league.

Now another crisis threatened. The two figures responsible for the club's administration were leaving. Jeff Archer, an American living in the area, had left for Holland, and Barry Hitchcock, deputy manager of the Brunel Sports Centre, had taken a post at Surrey University. Even with Jeff and Barry, administration had been difficult. Rules were everywhere in the National League. The need to replace them (both the people and the rules) was urgent.

This was the gospel according to Salih. It was a story told with passion and charm. Salih always knew more about charm than cybernetics – a fact confirmed by the fact that his doctoral thesis had already taken six years, and had no end in sight. As it happened, the timing of his appeal was perfect. I was just about to take my final undergraduate examination, and I needed a 'cause'. Perhaps I needed to do something reckless. Either way, basketball fitted perfectly.

*   *   *

I was never young. For as long as I can remember, I have been an obsessive worrier. Since the age of 14, I had been fighting for some cause, whether environmental, charitable or political. On those rare occasions when contentment with life had settled in, supporting Rotherham United topped up my sense of injustice. By the time I was 18, I was going to be Prime Minister. That was why I had come to Brunel.

Brunel was a strange choice. No one from my school had ever been there. Then again, no one from my school had been to Oxford or Cambridge, and no one from my family to university of any description. Brunel was the only university to offer a sandwich course in politics, and I reasoned that the experience and contacts would hold me in good stead. In the unlikely event of my being accepted at Oxford or Cambridge, I would have been swamped by more confident and socially developed peers. In the much more likely event of my applying and not being successful, I would be ridiculed by my school peers. So I didn't bother. Brunel would be fine – and so it was.

Four years later, politics was losing its attraction. Topics of life changing importance when campaigning for them for a hobby seemed much less interesting when writing essays about them. The course had filled its promise of greater exposure to politics, and I was not sure that I liked what I saw. Politics was different in London to Yorkshire, and student politics different to politics of any other kind. Also, I seemed to be the only person left who believed in the Labour Party. In 1980, even the Labour Party didn't believe in the Labour Party any more.

I was stranded. I had developed my political skills early. Now I wasn't sure that I needed them. Other skills more commonly associated with boys in their late teens were less developed. I was scruffy, displayed a complete lack of style and showed no interest in music – the least 'cool' person you could expect to meet. I found, too, that the communication skills needed to address an audience of 50 politicos were not the same as those to impress a girl. Nor did I get much opportunity. Brunel in those days had a male to female ratio of about 10 to one.

As a social misfit, out of touch with my generation, with limited principles and a completely impractical outlook, I had two options. The civil service would have been ideal, but a full-time position in the Brunel Students Union was easier to obtain. Incredibly, a university with less than 3,000 students had 10 full-time elected student posts covering everything from running student entertainments to running the student printing service. The result was a campus full of badly printed posters, advertising badly planned concerts that made a horrendous financial loss, of which the elected finance officer was completely unaware until months later – by which time a new set of officials had been elected for year. The post to which I had been elected aimed to develop better *ween* Brunel and the external world. You could make a case – as Salih *uid most* eloquently – to include basketball in this agenda.

Better still, I *knew* something about basketball. My home town of Doncaster boasted one of England's top teams during the 1970s. I attended my first game at the age of 16. The visitors were Crystal Palace – one of two teams that Doncaster had never beaten. Palace were regular national champions due, so rumour had it, to their having four times more money than anyone else in the league, an aggressive and bullying attitude and the southern bias of the English Basket Ball Association (who were based in Leeds). Whatever the merits of these arguments, the game was fantastic – Palace won after two periods of overtime, the majority of the Doncaster team fouled out and the crowd were baying for blood, such was the injustice of it all. It was great entertainment, and it appealed to my need for a 'cause'. I was hooked.

I was a regular fan of the Doncaster Panthers during my last two years at school, and an intermittent one while at Brunel. The Panthers continued to chip away at the so called natural order of things. They eventually beat both Crystal Palace and their other main rivals, Embassy All Stars of Milton Keynes, but the feeling of being 'outsiders' remained strong. In 1979, the peak of Panthers achievement, they won both the National League and Cup. Unfortunately, the English Basket Ball Association had introduced a new system, in which this counted for virtually nothing. The 'National Champions' were decided by a single, four team, tournament at the end of the season. Doncaster lost in the semi-final. It was Crystal Palace who took their usual place in Europe as England's number one team.

So Salih's intervention could not have been better timed. Instead of celebrating the end of my exams in traditional fashion the following evening, I presented myself at what was to become the first of hundreds of basketball meetings over the next seven years. It remains the only occasion I can remember where basketball actually saved me money.

*   *   *

It wasn't a large gathering – about eight people, including Barry, whose impending move to Surrey University had provoked the crisis, Salih and other long standing players. In the best traditions of basketball, lack of numbers was compensated for by a combination of blind enthusiasm, over confidence and pure hype.

These people provided the off court team to take us through seven years of on court drama. Will was the business brains behind the operation. He ran the local pet shop. He also did a great line in duck whistles. Dave was a local resident, drawn in when his son had started to come to training. I never quite worked out what Dave did, but assumed that it was something to do with jewellery because he could always get cheap watches to sell next to the cans of coca-cola at the club shop. But then again, he also had contacts in the world of t-shirts, and produced an absolutely wicked tape of ducks marching along singing which we played continually before games to infuriate visiting teams. Ray, another long-standing player, obviously worked in sales because he took the lead in selling the idea to me and subsequently became the announcer at games. Then there was Brian, committed but a little more subdued than the rest. He was the club treasurer, and obviously used to being the bearer of bad tidings.

I had no idea how these guys performed on court, but they worked well off it. There was an answer for everything. Why had the team finished bottom of the league the previous season? Mostly bad luck, with lots of close games that just went the wrong way in the end. (In fact, the Ducks only got within 10 points of their opponents twice.) Why did no one come to watch? This was because the team had been given such short notice of their admission to the league that they had not been able to publicise themselves properly. What about money? A university like Brunel should be well placed to attract sponsorship. If only…

If only. I soon realised that, if the club had a hundred pounds for every time those words were used at its meetings then it would be richer than Crystal Palace. This is a characteristic of sports fans everywhere. It is the same kind of 'if only' that I still hear from Bert of Dagenham, when he rings the radio football phone-in to say that his perennial mid-table football team could win the Premiership if only the Board would invest in a striker who scored 30 goals a season, and a goalkeeper who didn't let any in. Bert, of course, overlooks three problems. One – any team which scores goals and doesn't concede any would win the Premiership. Two – those players don't exist. Three – if they did then they wouldn't be heading for his club in a hurry. But there's nothing wrong with dreaming. Dreaming is probably the biggest single reason why most of us get involved in sport.

I was quickly offered, and accepted, the position of Promotions Director. I had absolutely no idea what this entailed, but it was explained that the position was a very important one. In fact, the National League handbook was produced to demonstrate that it was one of only two positions that clubs *must* have – the other being a Secretary. According to EBBA rules, there was no obligation to have a chairman, finance officer or, for that matter, any players. But a promoter was essential.

On closer examination, the role seemed less glamorous. On match night, the handbook specified that the home promoter had to convene a pre-match meeting with the commissioner (of which more later) and the opposition promoter. This resolved critical business such as confirming that adequate space existed for the match officials to get changed, determining which direction the teams would play in the first half and, most important of all, where post match refreshments would be served. Even the decision about which way to play involved no knowledge of basketball. When I expressed doubts that my tactical knowledge might not be adequate I was told simply to play towards the clock in the second half. That was what everybody did.

Other functions of the promoter were to put bums on seats (preferably more than 93 of them) and to secure publicity and sponsorship. In 1980, success in the basketball world was thought to be achieved through a very simple formula. If you had a good sponsor, you would hire two strong overseas (invariably American) players who would score 80 per cent of your points, and perhaps pay expenses to some decent English players capable of passing the ball to them. If you had mega sponsorship, you would bully or otherwise persuade the authorities that several other American players were in fact British, and thus did not come under the limit of two overseas players. If you had no sponsorship, then you struggled. It was as simple as that.

Nonetheless, I accepted, and was immediately presented with my first income generating opportunity – a jar of scratch off lottery tickets. It held 500 in total, of which about 30 had been sold. It was carefully explained that the tickets cost 10p each, and that the top prize was £10. This was an essential element (the only element) in our summer fund raising strategy.

'That's fine'. I said. Let's just hope that the top prize doesn't go too soon'.

'It already has. It was third bloody ticket out. But don't worry. No one knows'.

And it was important that no one should. The next prize was a pound. Even the average post-exam student would quickly work out that this was hardly a worthwhile investment. So it was that the first of my many disreputable acts in basketball involved selling lottery tickets that I knew had no chance of winning the first, and only worthwhile, prize.

*   *   *

Jeff Archer, the exuberant American who had been the driving force behind the Ducks elevation into the league, had left a mixed legacy. On the one hand, a level of ambition that now looked unsustainable. On the other, despite the short notice of league admission, he had put in place some of the building blocks for future success. No one was quite sure what these were – but they certainly included a spectacular playing kit, specially imported from the States, which unlike most in the league had numbers randomly distributed from 21 to 41, rather than the more conventional 4 to 15. The Ducks had been a distinctive, if not distinguished, force in their first season. Moreover, that kit would last for years. Or so it was thought.

More important even than the kit, we had a home court, and a court that didn't have to be paid for. This really was an asset, but there was nothing inevitable about its continuance. As the team had become more successful, the proportion of players studying at the university had started to decline – only four or five had appeared for the club in its first National League season. As this balance shifted further, questions were bound to be asked about whether the club could expect the same financial treatment as student societies. All the more so since its main supporter within the Sports Centre, Barry Hitchcock, was about to leave.

To counter this threat, a decision had been taken to invite the Sports Centre director, Mike Brightwell, to become club chairman. The appointment had its critics. Mike often gave the impression of being the typical beer swilling sportsman, concerned only with his twin passions of rugby (where thanks to his organisation the Brunel squad toured the world) and climbing (where he had installed reputedly the best wall in south-east England), and was incapable of grasping wider issues.

Mike revelled in his reputation, but it proved to be a false one. He complained endlessly – about the amount of court time used, the mess we made, the lack of notice given, our endless capacity to go over time and much, much more. Whenever we *really* needed something from the Sports Centre, though, he came up trumps – often at the expense of his relations with other users, his staff and even the university authorities.

Armed with all of this information, I now felt able to take stock of the position that we had inherited. I wrote it down as follows:

Assets	Liabilities
Free Court	No money
Great Kit	No players
Great Scoreboard	No crowd
470 Lottery Tickets	No first prize

It was going to be a long, hard summer.

MACCLESFIELD MAN

Although I might manage to sell 470 unused lottery tickets, I knew nothing about the wider issues of marketing. Identifying this problem, and developing a strategy to solve it, were two quite different matters.

Management theories can be difficult to apply to real life, and dangerous when applied half-heartedly. Years after this story, I visited a professor known to be particularly challenged by administrative issues, and was amazed to find his desk absolutely clean. He proudly explained his new 'clean desk' policy, which provided that a desk should be clean at all times, except for the immediate papers being used. This had revolutionised his productivity over the past week. Impressed by this, I reminded him of the topic of our meeting, at which point he reluctantly went to his cupboard to find the relevant papers, only to be deluged by literally hundreds of documents – cleared from his desk in a completely uncoordinated manner – which fell from the top shelf. Chapter two of the theory, which concerned filing, would follow next week.

No surprise, then, that the management section of the Brunel library was unable to provide a ready made strategy to promote a national league basketball team. In fact, I came away with just one key lesson, and that was the importance of knowing exactly what I was trying to promote. The more I thought about this over my lunchtime pint, the more complex it became. I thought I could see how basketball could be marketed – but what about the Brunel Ducks within it? Surely we could not create the same impact as the 'big city' teams that even then operated in towns such as Birmingham. But – and perhaps this was the critical question – should we even be trying to?

*   *   *

'Why are we called the Ducks'?' I asked Salih, as we loyally opened a handful of lottery tickets over our lunch.

'Dunno, really. Lots of people had different ideas. Does it matter?'

'Might do. I'm thinking about our *image*.'

'Oh, well in *that* case', he said with a sudden sense of urgency, 'I think it's something to do with the university crest'.

It struck me that, during a year of applying to, and four more of studying at Brunel, I had never given the crest the attention that it deserved.

'*Does* the university crest have a duck on it? I've never noticed.'

'No. It has a swan. They look alike after a few beers, and one night someone got the two mixed up. It sort of stuck.'

So there we had it. But for a few pints of beer (probably quite a few, I imagined) we could have been plotting the elegant, smooth rise of the Brunel Swans. Instead, in a league full of Tigers, Leopards, Lions, Panthers and Wildcats, we were the Ducks. As if a jar of unsold lottery tickets (now down to 453 thanks to Salih and my generosity) wasn't bad enough.

But perhaps having a nickname that made us the laughing stock of the league might be no bad thing? Perhaps the last thing that basketball needed was another set of giants from the animal kingdom, with their over inflated expectations and egos. 'Ducks' were something quite different. Down to earth, honest, unconventional and fun – but still capable of catching the odd fish – small or large – unaware. Whatever else it said about us, 'Ducks' signified character. We were going to need that in abundance.

*   *   *

In the meantime, I needed a second opinion, and I decided to seek this within the game. The opportunity came with an invitation to the league annual meeting, to be held in Macclesfield at the end of the month. No one else showed any enthusiasm to attend, and I jumped at the chance. After all, I was Promotions Director. And the Students Union would pay my fare. My title was Vice-President External Affairs. You didn't get much more external than Macclesfield.

I made two discoveries at the Macclesfield summit. The first was that the basketball 'community' was a very insular one. Everyone knew everyone's business, largely because everyone else wanted them to. In part, this was just another aspect of competition. It was good to be in the limelight, and everyone wanted to show that they were about to sign a new player, new sponsor or new deal of some kind.

In part, though, the community aspect was genuine. In 1980 (as today) few people had seen the potential of basketball in Britain. Those who had done were drawn together, whether they liked it or not. Running a National League basketball team could dominate your life. The more you knew your co-owners, the more you combined outward civility with the desire to put one over on them.

Being a member of this community was *not* the same as having friends. I still have my diary for 1987, my last year of involvement in basketball. It contains almost three hundred telephone numbers. Of these, over two thirds were entirely or mainly connected with basketball. I guess my diary for, say 1990, contained only about five of these. There are only three that I see, even rarely, today. It was a sad commentary on an activity that dominated my life for seven years, and quite unlike any other phase of my life.

Basketball became obsessive. The desire to win, or at least survive, in our new found community made us do incredible things. At least one club owner went to jail for activities related to basketball. Others were concerned that their basketball involvement might call into question their status as a fit and proper person to run other companies. This was the tip of the iceberg. There were more 'prats per acre' in basketball than any other walk of life that I have ever encountered. Did these people behave in the same way in the remainder of their lives? I never heard of any being murdered, so I assume not.

My second discovery about the basketball community was how transitory it was. I was one of several 'newcomers' at the Macclesfield meeting, and there were fresh cohorts at every annual meeting for the following seven years. This influx was not a sign of expansion. Newcomers came in because established teams were dropping out. A glance at the league tables over the past 30 years of British Basketball shows an alarming rate of turnover. Well over a hundred teams have appeared in the National League over the past three decades. Supporters were transitory, too. Basketball's key market was parents looking for somewhere to take their kids, or sixth formers and students looking for a cheap date on a Saturday night. It was something that you grew out of. British Basketball did not inspire lifelong allegiances in the same way that football does.

These discoveries made it easy to ask other club promoters for advice. Basketball might be competitive, but egos were high. Everyone loved to be asked how they did things, and no one was in the least surprised to find a newcomer asking them. As always in basketball, there was no shortage of people willing to speak. The need was to be selective.

From watching the Doncaster Panthers, I realised that the most successful teams on the court were not the most successful at promoting themselves. Crystal Palace, for all their string of titles, routinely played their home games before empty houses. Doncaster had created a good atmosphere, but only filled their relatively small court on special occasions. From a promotional point of view, the team that impressed me most was Team Granwood of Coventry. They appeared to have a stable sponsor, an enthusiastic crowd and a full stadium. They even played some home games on a university campus, at the University of Warwick.

Bob Hope was the team promoter, and most other things besides. Surprisingly, he did not feel that his thoroughly professional organisation, one of the top four clubs in England, would be in the least bit threatened by a bunch of students whose accidental national league career had started so painfully. He offered to help in any way that he could. He invited me to his office but, time and resources being what they were, I followed up with a phone call (from the Students Union, naturally) instead.

I recall one comment, in particular. We were talking about how to attract advertisers and sponsors, or indeed even getting them to even talk to us. Bob understood the problem. Most of us, he said, are bound by the rules that apply in 'real' life. If someone says 'no', you tend to take it that this is what they mean. You don't like to argue, and you certainly don't want to beg – so you leave it and move on. In the world of sponsorship, this approach is doomed to failure. The only way to be effective is to assume that, even if your initial target says no, or is unwilling to speak to you, then someone else will.

The solution was to remember the simple fact that, even if your approach is ultimately unsuccessful, you will *never* see or speak to the person on the other end of the telephone again. Even if you should, by coincidence, meet them in another capacity, they will have no idea who you are. In short, the people that you are approaching are not really part of your life, and not subject to your normal standards of pride and politeness. Remember that, and your level of persistence will quickly increase. This turned out to be brilliant advice – all the more so since it was free.

*   *   *

Before unleashing the Ducks on the unsuspecting business community of Uxbridge, the Macclesfield meeting had thrown up an even more urgent problem. One of the few assets of the club was already under threat, with a proposal to ensure that, in future, all teams should have kit numbered from 4 to 15. This would, of course, render our high quality US kit, a key legacy of the Archer – Hitchcock era – useless. Resistance was imperative.

To understand this proposal, it is necessary to understand the mentality of the English Basket Ball Association. In 1980 the EBBA was faced with the challenge of expanding basketball in a way that satisfied and encouraged investment at the 'professional end' of the sport, while reassuring local league clubs and players that basketball was still 'their' game. Everyone agreed that they were getting this balance wrong – few on how to get it right.

The desire to expand the size, popularity and profile of the league was genuine but, as with the decision to reject, and then admit the Ducks to the league in the first place, external events often span out of their control. National League Basketball was subject to constraints that were well beyond the jurisdiction of the Association.

Basketball is potentially the best spectator sport in the world. It is athletic, exciting, fast and free scoring. The rules are such that, at the basic level, everyone can understand them, and at an advanced level, even the match officials cannot. So everyone has an opinion, and does not hesitate to express it. It is played in warm, clean and relatively comfortable conditions – a factor even more important in the 1980s than today. It had no hooligan element. Not among the fans, at least.

The key to realising this potential was equality of competition. In football, a team winning a game by six clear goals can be exciting (at least for supporters of the winning team). In basketball, a game won by 30 or 40 points is boring. All too often, the result is a forgone conclusion after the first five minutes, the strongest players are withdrawn and the rest of the game is pedestrian. As Crystal Palace had found to their cost, even teams that produced such results each week could not guarantee a worthwhile following.

In an ideal world, the strategy for the league would have been to promote equality between its members, perhaps through a US style drafting system or wage caps, and then, perhaps, to seek out venues that could hold more than a thousand or so spectators, to cope with this increased demand. This was never likely in English basketball. We had all come into the game to promote our own teams, interests, and, most of all, our own egos. The aim was to win. Promoting the wider sport would help this, but it was very much a by-product. In any case, the very top teams justified their special position by arguing that it was in the interests of English basketball that its top teams should complete strongly in Europe. This was an argument on which the EBBA – like today's football authorities – constantly placed too much weight.

Unable to influence the large issues, the EBBA focussed on the small ones. What better place to start than shirt numbers? Ensuring that each team had a roster from 4 to 15 would be neat and tidy. It would add a degree of consistency, and help fans and media, who were obviously incapable of understanding any number over 20, to understand the game. Brilliant! And here was I, metaphorically speaking, sat on one kit, designed to be so unlike any other in the league that colour clashes were never an issue, which had no number 4, 7 and 10, but proudly displayed numbers 21, 22, 23, 33 and 41.

How to avert this crisis? Over the next seven years, I found that there were essentially four arguments that could be used be fight off EBBA regulation. These can be defined as naivety, ignorance, poverty and diversion. Any of these could have applied to the Macclesfield situation, but I was too naive to realise this. So naivety was the order of the day.

I intervened, in a matter of fact way, to apologise for not having seen the proposed regulation before (not that anyone else had), but that we had an almost new strip bearing different numbers, which had been given to us, and that changing now would not only cost money, but offend a valued donor. I stressed that I personally had no strong feelings about what numbers should be worn – come to think of it, who else, except the EBBA, could *possibly* have strong feelings about shirt numbers? Of course, we expected to have a new sponsor before long, and at that point we expected to change our main kit anyway.

The last point proved to be the clincher. *Everybody* expected to have a new sponsor before long in public, and everyone equally knew that most of us would not get one. My naivety rating soared. The intervention was harmless. It had been a long meeting and no one wanted to argue. An exemption was agreed for those teams that already had kit bearing different numbers, on condition that any future kit conformed. After all, how long could a kit last?

I was grateful that this, my only intervention in the meeting, had been met with such a sympathetic response, and sat back in the knowledge that my return fare to Macclesfield had been repaid several times over. Not that I, or the club, had paid for it of course.

THE REAGAN EFFECT

Two chapters into this book, not a single ball has been thrown, passed or shot in anger. This reflects something about my own role. I knew nothing about the tactics of the game. In any event, I was too busy selling lottery tickets and completing forms from the English Basket Ball Association to notice such trivia.

Things were happening, none the less. Following Barry's defection, the team needed a new coach, and a volunteer arrived in the form of Tony Harrison, who at the grand old age of 30ish was no older than some of the players, but had been around a bit. Well, as far as the exotically named See-N-See Sonics of Maidenhead to the West, and Avenue of Edmonton to the East. Neither team still existed, but with such a cosmopolitan existence, Coach Tony had obviously come across other potential players who were experienced and, critically, free. One or two of these were brought in to add to the squad.

The 'American problem' had also been solved without undue cost. Jeff Johnson, who had joined from the ill-fated Maidenhead team at the start of the previous season, had been found a job in the Sports Centre. A search of local US air bases had found Mike McLarin – who like all American military personnel was shrouded in mystery, but did have security clearance to reveal that he was 6ft 4in tall, had a great jump shot and by common consent among my three female acquaintances, a wicked smile. He and Jeff made an impressive combination, at least off the court. My earliest vision of them together is of Mike driving them down the M23 to a pre-season tournament in Brighton, in an open top car, beer in hand, evidently without a care in the world.

The most significant retention from the previous season was guard and eventual team captain, Phil Ralfe. When this story goes to Hollywood, Phil will be the hero figure. In a sport where change was the norm, and loyalty of any kind a rarity, Phil was a virtual ever present throughout this story, moving from exciting young prospect to grand old man of the squad.

Phil will be the ideal subject for our Hollywood producer. He worked in computers, at a time when computers were fashionable. He had a flat in Harrow, when Harrow was fashionable. His girlfriends, all of whom played basketball, were very fashionable indeed. None of these aspects of his life ever seemed to distract Phil from playing basketball, and particularly playing for Brunel. In 1982, at a time when everyone in the sport was being dazzled by the prospect of fame and fortune that regular television would bring, Phil told *Basketball Monthly* that 'we don't want to miss the boat now. If I wasn't good enough to play in the First Division, I'd play in the second team'. I could never understand why Phil was such an exception – perhaps it was the lure of being the only person in the league entitled to wear a number-23 shirt. Whatever the reason, we were all very grateful.

*   *   *

Our object for the season was consolidation. In fact, that was the only objective possible, since everyone knew who was going to win the division from the outset. A new club, Solent Stars, had been formed under the ownership of Harry Smith, a self-made millionaire. For once, the title reflected the team – All Stars had, indeed, been recruited from throughout the UK game and elsewhere. There had, of course, been a campaign for such an eminent team to bypass the trivia of the second division altogether and be elevated straight to the first. Surprisingly – but rightly – this was rejected. Fortunately, the Ducks fixture list revealed that this particular problem would not hit us until late November.

The league had expanded to nine teams, all of the others bring kitted out with boring uniformity in pristine uniforms numbered 4–15, in line with the Macclesfield proclamation. Despite the gusto of the Macclesfield meeting, few had acquired the expected sponsorship deals. One exception to this was Leeds, now revelling in the title of National Breakdown Leeds, and thus establishing a tradition of West Yorkshire teams whose sponsors saddled them with ridiculous names. In later years, this embraced Calderdale Explorers and Bradford Mythbreakers, both sponsored by their local tourist authorities. We were just pleased that Heckmondwike and Hebden Bridge didn't merge and start a team. The printing bill would have been huge.

Happily, Uxbridge did not have a tourism authority desperate to bring its charms to a wider audience. The idea of Uxbridge Stopovers taking on Bradford Mythbreakers may have been too much even for the basketball authorities. The student market did have its attractions, however, and several match sponsors were recruited. The first of these was Endsleigh, the student based insurance company, who paid the princely sum of £400 to sponsor our first home league game of the season, against Nottingham.

It looked a great deal for both parties. For us, this was the equivalent of selling 4,000 lottery tickets. Even more in the unlikely event that any of them won a prize. For Endsleigh it represented, to quote my proposal 'a unique opportunity to access the valuable student market at a critical time in the year'. What could possibly go wrong?

What went wrong was that both parties assumed that the other knew something about sponsorship. For us, it was a fair assumption. Endsleigh was a national brand, it had an office on campus and lots of attractive glossy leaflets that had presumably been designed and printed by *someone*. For Endsleigh, leaving this high profile strategic assignment to the Eric, the youngest and least inexperienced recruit in their sales department proved to be a mistake of heroic proportions.

Those glossy leaflets were at the heart of the problem. Ensdsleigh – or at least Endsleigh Eric – was very proud of their glossy leaflets. In fact, they had produced six, each to describe a separate product. Perhaps we should have realised this when, in our sponsorship proposal, we promised that 'every student on campus would receive information about the full range of Endsleigh products.' The enormity of the error did not strike home until the day before the game when, instead of taking delivery of delivery of 2,000 leaflets, we were faced with 12,000. Box, after box, after box. Behind the boxes came Endsleigh Eric.

Many students lived together in flats of five or six rooms. Did this mean, we asked, that every flat should have six copies of the leaflets – all six leaflets? Endsleigh Eric thought hard. Yes, on balance he thought it did. Leaflets, he had been told, had a conversion rate of two per cent into new business. The more leaflets, the more business. It was a pretty simple concept, and in any event, we had promised. It was there in black and white.

*　　*　　*

Friday 10 October 1980 was a day when determination ruled over common sense. In Brighton, Prime Minister Margaret Thatcher told the Conservative Party conference that, despite the desperate state of the economy, there would be no U-turn in Government policy. 'The Lady', she famously declared, was 'not for turning'. In Uxbridge, a small band of Brunel Ducks supporters were defying logic in a similarly determined fashion. By lunchtime, each flat on the Brunel campus had been treated to a deluge of 36 leaflets, each describing one of six products, not to mention a handful of humble discount vouchers for the game.

It is possible that some recipients gathered this important documentation, took it to the kitchen, laid it out on the table, and carefully divided it between the residents. Sadly, this was not the typical reaction. Students have never been at the forefront of anti litter campaigns, and in 1980 recycling was something that took place only when there was a dead heat in the Tour de France. By early evening, the campus was awash with Endsleigh leaflets.

What effect this had on Endsleigh sales is not recorded. Strangely it had a big impact on the Ducks. To our astonishment, over 400 eager eyed students presented themselves and their discount vouchers on the following evening. Only a handful had come to enquire which idiot had reduced their pristine living conditions to a paper chase. It was the biggest crowd in the history of the Brunel Ducks, by a very wide margin.

The team had started credibly – with an expected defeat at Brighton, a win at newcomers Colchester (our main 'target' if we were to avoid bottom spot again), and a more surprising victory over Camden in the National Cup. Nottingham was the biggest test yet. Having won the league in the previous season, they had either been refused promotion, or decided not to take it.

Basketball had not yet absorbed the concept that a team that won the second division would start the following season in the first. The idea was resisted with a range of arguments similar to those used 70 years earlier to delay giving women the vote. It would preserve standards – both on court and off. It was in the interests of the candidate teams themselves, who might be out of place in the new environment. It would prevent anarchy. Far better, for all concerned, if the decision were made by a group of anonymous chaps sat around a committee table.

It was difficult for teams like Nottingham to decide whether they *wanted* promotion. There was a real gap between the first and second division, not only in playing standards but at all levels of organisation. Basketball was not a game given to shocks. In football, a sub-standard team promoted to a higher division is likely to win at least a handful of games. In basketball, they are likely to lose week, after week, after week, a demoralising experience for all concerned. On the other hand, teams need to have something to aim for. If the opportunity is not taken, the best that can happen is a repeat of the previous season. Without ambition, it becomes hard to motivate players, supporters and sponsors alike.

Promotion was the last thing on our mind. Marketing Nottingham as the reigning champions was our way of telling the world that we were the underdogs, and that they should not expect too much. This looked to be just as well, because we were four points down in the first minute. Even when half-time arrived with Brunel leading by six, the prevailing view was that it could never last. As the second half progressed, it dawned on us only gradually that it might. The lead reached 11 points with five minutes left, but started to ebb away. As nerves frayed, the foul count rose. Nottingham won eight free throws in the last minute alone. The seventh of these levelled the scores at 83 all, with seven seconds left. Amidst high excitement, the next one was missed. Even so, the lead had gone, and there were no draws in basketball. No one gave much for the Ducks' prospects in extra-time.

Cometh the hour, cometh the man. It was all too easy to see teams like Brunel as being dependent on two Americans. Only seven of the 10 man Brunel squad got on to court during the Nottingham game. All the points came from four players. 64 of the 84 came from Jeff and Mike. But at the end of the day the spotlight fell squarely on one of the English players. Having held possession tenuously for six and a half of the last seven seconds, one of the Brunel players was fouled. That player was Bob Hill.

I don't really remember Bob Hill. He had been a regular during the previous season, but was to play only three more league games for the Ducks. I remember him very clearly, however, going all alone to the free throw line, under a clock which showed no seconds at all left, to take three free throws. Because basketball is obsessed with statistics, and because I still have my 1981–82 *Basketball Review,* I can tell you that Bob took 83 free throws in his national league career, with a rather ordinary success rate of 53 per cent. I doubt if he remembers any of them more clearly than these three. I can still hear the groan when the first shot bounced out, and the roar when the second one rolled round the ring and dropped through the basket. The third one missed, but no one cared. Thirteen months after joining the National League, Brunel had its first home win, by the narrowest of margins. And Bob Hill had his place in club history.

We caught the mood by staging a friendly the following week – a relatively uneventful win against non-league Oxford. So by mid October, the Ducks had four successive wins. It was their best ever run (by a margin of three) and this basketball lark was beginning to seem easy. Drown the campus in leaflets, and the students flood in. The players all respond by performing out of their skins, and everyone goes home happy. It was a simple strategy, but devastating in its effect. Even a heavy defeat against first division Kingston didn't dampen spirits. If anything, it confirmed our audacity in getting to the second round of the Cup in the first place. Our next league game was at home, too. We could hardly wait.

*   *   *

Our next potential victims, Wolverhampton, duly arrived. So did another healthy crowd, players, officials and even Norman, a friendly journalist from the *Uxbridge Gazette* who acquired a habit of bringing his dog to matches. In fact, by half past seven, everyone had arrived – except for star player Mike. All was explained in a hurried phone call. Mike was being held by the police.

He explained, with a degree of understatement untypical of his compatriots, that it was nothing serious. He had been travelling to the game from his air base near Oxford, and had to change trains at Slough. What happened next we are not certain, but the outcome was that he was being held by police for 'acting suspiciously'. He needed someone to vouch for him – and quickly. Will was nominated on three grounds. He had the biggest car, lived just outside Slough and he could talk. We reckoned that anyone who could sell hamsters day after day was probably our best hope of rescuing an innocent basketball player.

With more time to plan, the arrest could have provided huge political credibility for the Ducks. The 'sus' law, under which Mike was evidently being detained, was the subject of huge controversy at the time, allowing as it did for police to stop anyone just on the grounds that they looked as though they might, sometime and somewhere unspecified, do something not very nice. Basketball players fitted the profile perfectly – big, black, young and inarticulate. Properly marketed, the arrest could have turned the Ducks from being the latest diversionary tactic of capitalist society to being at the forefront of the revolution. The experience served to confirm that the law was either racist or stupid. Mike's colour may or not have contributed to his arrest, but the idea that he was less trustworthy than Will, his appointed rescuer, was stretching the bounds of credibility to their limit.

Will did his job brilliantly, but time was of the essence, both in Slough and at Brunel. We were playing our part. At ten to eight, the match ball vanished. Five minutes later, there was a scoreboard fault. At the scheduled start time, we felt obliged to make some minor queries regarding the team lists. We even discussed turning the lights out altogether, but for once discretion ruled. All of this gained us a miserable six minutes, and in only my fifth appearance as promoter, my first threat of a fine.

It also fired up the opposition, and after starting the game with undue haste at 20.06, things went from bad to worse. By the ninth minute Ducks had conceded 19 successive points to trail by 21–6 and had, naturally, used both of their first half-time outs in a further attempt to delay matters. During the second of these, McLarin arrived. Entering the game immediately, and with no warm up, he quickly attracted three free throws – and missed them all. He contributed just one basket in the rest of the first half, and half-time arrived with Ducks still trailing by 13 points.

If the Slough police were still looking for evidence against McLarin, they could have done worse than look at his half-time drink. Whatever it contained, it made all the difference. Brunel scored the first 12 points of the second half, McLarin 10 of them. It didn't settle the issue; in fact the lead changed seven times during the half, but it was a crucial turning point. Brunel entered the last minute three points ahead, won back possession and McLarin was fouled. He completed what was, to say the least, a mixed evening on a high note, by sinking both. Brunel won by 84–79. We were now third in the league, and the crowd loved it.

*   *   *

In fact, sufficient numbers loved it to ensure a full coach (players included) for the next game, away to National Breakdown Leeds in the palatial surroundings of the Batley Leisure Centre. The idea of supporters travelling on the same coach as the players was a novel one. Purists will argue that they could get in the way, harass the players or disturb their pristine pre-match preparation. I took a less sophisticated view. The supporters each paid two pounds – two pounds that we wouldn't otherwise have. Thirty times £2 was £60 and that, for say eight away games a year, was a tangible part of our budget. The choice was not one between a full bus and an empty bus, but a full bus and no bus at all. Some years later, the policy was described in a national basketball supporters' magazine as giving the club 'a unique family atmosphere'. Well, there was that, too.

We lost at Batley – the margin that could hardly have been worse had we all walked there. This, though, was only one of our worries. The departure of Mike, who fouled out of the game four minutes into the second half, proved to be the end of his short lived and successful partnership with Jeff. Apart from one game, it was also the last occasion we were able to field two 'Americans' all season.

Having an American player from a US base had one obvious advantage. It was cheap. There were also drawbacks. First, there was no way that a base player could be under contract. Second, a base player could not always give notice of what he would be doing next week. Many could not even say what they were doing *last* week. Such was the case with Mike – even without extra obstacles provided by the Slough constabulary.

History records that on 4 November 1980, Ronald Reagan was elected as the 40th President of the United States. Immediately afterwards Mike McLarin, employee of the US government, disappeared from the score sheets of the Brunel Ducks. It would be remiss not to ask how far this was really coincidence.

The historical case against Reagan (on this issue, at least) looks tenuous. Set against the wider problems of the world, it is slightly doubtful that Reagan's first thought on election was to determine the availability of his air force employees for basketball games three thousand miles away. In any event, Reagan didn't take up his post until the following January, and it later transpired that Mike had picked up an injury. But these were the eighties. Conspiracy theories were rife and, as we had found only a fortnight before, this was an age in which people could incur suspicion just by *looking* guilty. Republican Presidents had a long standing suspicion of involving the US military in conflicts that didn't involve them. Added to all of this, the gallery of posters that covered the Student Union confirmed that Reagan was the enemy of underdogs the world over. Brunel Ducks were certainly underdogs. You had to wonder…

*   *   *

Whatever the reason, Mike's disappearance could not have come at a worse time. Our next game was the long dreaded clash with the all conquering Solent Stars. Faced with the dilemma of attracting a big crowd for a match which had only one possible end, we resorted to the now well rehearsed tactic of lowering expectations. The full page article promoting the game in the Brunel student newspaper couldn't have been more explicit. Solent had beaten two first division teams already, they had not been held to a margin of less than 20 points in any league game, and had recently recorded a league record victory margin of 70 points against Wolverhampton. They had also just set a British record transfer fee, signing Crystal Palace star Mark Saiers for a 'massive' £15,000, one of four front line players and a coach who previously played for the champions. In short, our message was that 'this will be interesting, but we *are* going to get panned. Please come and support us – but you have been warned'.

The crowd duly showed up, and we filled our part of the bargain. The game turned out to be the most one sided in national league history. Some teams would get 20 points ahead, relax and let the game peter out. Solent paid their opponents the complement of giving 100 per cent commitment throughout. Rather too much so, I couldn't help but feel. We were eight points down in the first three minutes; 20 by half-time, 30 by five minutes into the second half, 40 just three minutes later and 50 in another two minutes. By the end we had racked up a shattering 50–121 defeat, beating the humiliation of Wolverhampton by a single point. We were record breakers.

Football managers always point to the 'positives' to emerge from disastrous defeats. In fact, the game marked the debut of a new player – Ian Hunt, a newly arrived student in London. Remarkably, he decided to stay. Sadly, though, it was also a final appearance. Unknown to any of us, Jeff Johnson had been approached with a better offer to play in Holland. No one could have doubted his commitment in his last game, when he had contributed 24 of the Ducks'

50 points, but the fact remained that within three weeks we had gone from two Americans to no Americans.

The next three weeks were not a comfortable experience. Only six players had been available to make the trip to Liverpool, and the availability of over seven seats each on the full size coach was little consolation. We lost by 50 odd, and then by 30 odd to Camden. Harold Wilson once said that a week was a long time in politics. In basketball a month was beginning to seem like an eternity.

We had seen the very best and very worst of basketball, all within two months. We hoped that the norm was somewhere in the middle. In the short-term, our future as a National League club was on the line. Even more immediately than that, we had the problem of how many players would show up for the final game of the year, the visit of Brighton to Brunel, five days before Christmas. Thankfully enough turned up not only to fill the bench, but hold a top three team to a margin of just five points. Crisis averted.

* * *

Christmas is a time for reflection. 1980 gave us more to reflect on than most years. On 8 December the world was shocked by the assassination of John Lennon. America had its most hawkish president for decades. Russia announced two nuclear tests. Iran added to the global sense of insecurity by demanding a huge ransom for 417 American hostages, who were in turn remembered throughout America on Christmas Eve, by ceremonies of shining lights for 417 seconds. It was a time for serious, sober thinking. Britons responded by turning out in their millions to put a school choir rendition of *There's no one Quite Like Grandma* top of the Christmas charts.

Insofar as I reflected about basketball, I reckoned that the pluses of the past six months just about outweighed the minuses. We had already won more games than the previous season, and proved that we could attract both crowds and sponsors. If anyone doubted the latter, there were still enough Endsleigh leaflets floating around to prove the point. In other ways, though, nothing had changed. Consolidation had been our aim at the start of the season. Three months later, consolidation was needed more than ever.

Consolidation was just about what the second half of the season delivered. Mathematics professors, incurable optimists and obsessive anoraks like me could take satisfaction in a 20 per cent improvement in our return game against Solent (we only lost by 56), calculate that the return against Liverpool had seen a 60 per cent improvement in the margin, and become positively ecstatic at an 80 per cent narrowing of the gap against Camden. To the outside world, such niceties were less important. We had still lost those three games by a combined total of over 80 points. The casual observer could be forgiven for thinking that, after the early season flurry, normal service had been resumed.

*   *   *

Well, the casual observer was wrong, because a lot was happening in the early part of 1981. First, our players stayed – all six of them! Second, Mike made a brief re-appearance from the start of the year until – suspiciously – the week of Ronald Reagan's inauguration, but long enough to help ensure wins in the return games against Colchester and Wolverhampton. We thus held on to the dizzy heights of seventh place in the final table – our best position ever!

Third, showing a rare and total disregard for financial caution, we splashed out on a transfer fee for a player. Not that we meant to. When Coach Tony announced that Richard Parsons, recently graduated from the junior squad at nearby Hemel, wanted to join us, we were mildly pleased. When we heard that he was 6ft 9in tall, we were delighted. When we heard that Hemel would require a transfer fee we were astonished, but it was too late to change our mind. I remember vaguely that we were asked for £500. I remember precisely that we offered absolutely nothing. After arbitration, we agreed on £100.

On the one hand, this was a cost item that I deeply resented. On the other, it could have been worse. 1981 saw the British record for a football transfer fee reach £1,500,000, when Brian Robson moved to Manchester United. In historical terms, we were back in 1893 – year of the first ever £100 transfer fee paid by Aston Villa for one Willie Groves. Moreover, Willie only played for Villa for just over a year, before leaving after a contract dispute; Richard played for us for almost three years, at an estimated cost of about £2.50 per game. And while Villa didn't learn from their mistakes, and continued to pay ever increasing transfer fees for the following 90 years, we certainly did. Richard's remains our record (indeed our only) transfer fee to this day.

Finally, January saw us come closer than ever to recruiting our first 'real'

American. Not that Jeff and Mike hadn't been real – in the sense that they had two arms, two legs and (between them) two American passports. But they were not 'our' Americans in the sense that they had not come to the UK specially to play basketball for us. Vaughan, a friend of someone who knew someone else who knew someone at Brunel, arrived in late January and really did come to play basketball. There was only one element missing in the perfect scenario. We didn't actually pay him. But he did stay with Salih, who in turn pressurised us into meeting the odd food bill, so we were getting very close.

Given his somewhat unsatisfactory terms of engagement, Vaughan was incredibly committed, friendly and tolerant, and much more effective on court than we had any right to expect. He even seemed quite proud to be a (sort of) full-time basketball player. Two years later we saw him on a visit to Washington. He told us how proud his mother had been of this status, and how she had tried to persuade him to return for the following season. I don't think he had the heart to tell her that we hadn't been able to actually pay for his services.

Vaughan brought stability at a time when things could easily have fallen apart. This allowed me, still clinging to the belief that it was possible to combine basketball with other areas of life, to retire for a brilliant summer in which Rotherham were promoted, England won the ashes in spectacular fashion, the Thatcher government stumbled from crisis to crisis and I earned my first real salary cheque as an academic. There was a royal wedding, too.

BRAVE NEW WORLD

People had all kinds of ideas in 1981. Some were better than others. It was the year that saw the first personal computer and the launch of the Social Democratic Party. It was a year in which it was more important to do something quickly than to do something sensible. Even the Royal family sprang into action. In February, Prince Charles became engaged. In July, he was married. By November, he was going to be a father. Action was the order of the day.

The most immediate action on my agenda was to find the means to eat. My post with the students union had only been for one year, and in any event had been such a success that it had been abolished. To the chagrin of the far left, far right, aspiring entertainment moguls, printers and others who just fancied a paid year away from the real labour market, our Student Union Executive abolished six of the 10 sabbatical officer posts. The Students Union, I remember declaring to a sceptical general meeting, would never be the same again. For a start, it would be solvent. The Union President at that time went on to be Finance Director of a top company. I, by contrast, seemed destined to be the Brunel Labour Club's equivalent of Ramsay McDonald.

I left my post in the Students Union four months early, having surprisingly been offered a six months research post in my old department, thus achieving the distinction of leaving a short term position for an even shorter one. I combined this with research work for a Labour Member of Parliament, at a time when the effectiveness of the Parliamentary Labour Party was showing disturbing similarities with that of the English Basket Ball Association.

A more permanent solution was needed by October, and there were two options. In April, I was offered a government funded doctoral studentship, again at Brunel. All seemed settled until, one morning in August I received a call from the University of Warwick, where I had applied to undertake a Masters course in Industrial Relations, to say that they could also offer me a funded place.

It should have been a tough call. Industrial Relations was a growth area in a country whose last two governments had been toppled by a failure to keep the peace, and whose current one seemed unlikely to fare any better. Warwick was probably the strongest course in the country. On the other hand Warwick would require me to move, offered only one further year's refuge from the labour market and, surprisingly, had no built-in option to help run a basketball team. As with just about every other career move in my life, my decision was made within seconds. I was grateful, but would stay at Brunel.

Maybe, too, there was another reason. Every Hollywood blockbuster needs a love interest, and in my case this was Carol. It isn't easy to introduce her because, quite frankly, I can't remember when and where we first met. She always just seemed to be *there* – on my course, in the library, at student union meetings, in the pub. It gradually dawned on me, with all the perception of the typical male, that I was glad she was. By 1981, we were, well, *friends.* By 1982, we were friends who rented a house together for the sake of convenience. By 1983, friends who slept together for the first time because our basketball team manager assumed that we did and booked us into a double room by mistake. By 1984, friends who bought a flat together, partly out of affection but partly, we insisted, for investment reasons. By 1985, friends who agreed to get married, and by 1986 friends who had the same name. To anyone in the outside world, this must have seemed like watching paint dry. To me, it was love. She wouldn't admit it in public, but Carol actually became quite committed to the Ducks cause, and her determination not to be outwitted was every bit as strong as mine. I wouldn't admit it, but her presence at Brunel probably saved the world from producing yet another personnel manager.

∗   ∗   ∗

Studying for a doctorate and running a basketball club are the most compatible positions in the world. As Salih demonstrated, there was no real expectation that a PhD would ever finish. It seems incredible today, but of the doctoral students funded by the (then) Social Sciences Research Council in 1976, only 11 per cent had completed them within four years. My supervisor subscribed strongly to the self-help philosophy. He popped his head around the door on my first day to reassure me that he only took on postgraduate students that he felt could do the job themselves, and would not be hassling him unduly. Added to this, I was the only 'full-time' doctoral student in my entire department. Independence was very much the order of the say. That suited me fine.

The first milestone for my doctorate was a literature survey and report. This was expected by June 1982. The basketball season, by contrast, was due to start on 26 September 1981. Somehow, the needs of basketball seemed more urgent. Last year we could write off as a learning exercise. Now, we reasoned, we had seen all the pitfalls. We were experienced.

Coach Tony continued his strategy of boosting the squad with players from elsewhere in the area, gradually helped by the fact that we were making a fist of league membership. Not superstars, or players that you would have heard of, and certainly not players who would require any money – Ian Cohen had played for Colchester, who had the distinction of replacing us at the bottom of the league, Bob Senior had moved to the area having studied in Exeter. Bob Spencer seemed to have played everywhere. Well, at least everywhere from Oxford to Hemel. We were becoming a cosmopolitan bunch.

Then there was Nigel. Nigel was a refugee from a dispute between his own club, the Watford Royals, and his former one, the nearby Division One Team Hemel Hempstead. This story said the world about basketball. The precise details are unfathomable, but I have pieced together my version, with the help of *Pawprint,* an anorak's website which meticulously charted the history of some 130 clubs that have drifted in and out of the National League since its inception. This reads as follows:

'Hemel Lakers entered the National Basketball League in 1977. Watford Royals were already an established local club. In 1981, Watford applied to join the league, and were accepted, but then had their place withdrawn following objections from Hemel. The following year, this decision was reversed, and Watford Royals entered the league. In 1984, the two clubs merged, playing as Hemel and Watford Royals, but by 1986 Hemel were once again just Hemel (although this time Hemel Royals) and by 1989 Watford were back in the league, now called Watford Rebels. The same year, Hemel (still Royals), who in 1988 had opted to join the recently established British Basketball League from the National Basketball League, opted to leave it. They rejoined the British League in 1990, only to be relegated, but reinstated, in 1992. Watford (Rebels), on the other hand, had won promotion in 1990, but now moved to Ware where they played until moving to Stevenage, to be replaced by another Ware team (Ware Fire) who then adopted the previous name of Ware Rebels, and merged with a group of supporters from the former London Leopards team to become Essex and Herts Leopards, which played home games at three different venues before returning to Ware. In the meantime Hemel Royals once again became Hemel and Watford Royals, and moved to Watford Leisure Centre, which had been the original home of Watford Royals, with whom they should not be confused. A year later, they moved to Milton Keynes, to become Milton Keynes Lions, where they should definitely not be confused with two previous clubs to play in Milton Keynes. Nor, obviously, should either club be confused with Westfield Watford Storm, a later incarnation from the West Herts Warriors, which came about when the West Herts first team were placed by the league authorities one division lower than their second team'.

Got all that? Good. Underlying this saga are tales that would have the potential to rival any American soap opera, were it not for the almost complete absence of any real power or money. That, moreover, is just the story of the men's teams. Hertfordshire women's basketball deserves a chapter to itself.

Nigel, a former Hemel player, had been instrumental in Watford's application to join the league. When the acceptance had been reversed, he showed no inclination to return to the club that had been the chief objectors. Instead he was determined on revenge.

So there was nothing to be done but to take advantage. Travelling back from the obscure motorway hotels that hosted league meetings I had broached the idea that he might join us, at least until Watford managed to cut their way through the layers of indecision and self-interest that constituted the league admission procedure. He thought he might, providing that we continued to support Watford's cause and would not charge a transfer fee if and when he wanted to move back. These were two conditions that showed how well he had got to know me.

*   *   *

We still had to resolve the issue of two foreign players, and how to pay for them. Financially, our strategy was to put as high proportion of our funds as possible into players and the essentials of getting them on court. The definition of what we considered essential was unbelievably narrow. Not only did we make the same kit last for five years, but in the same period we didn't own more than a dozen balls. Collecting them at the end of each game and training session was like a military operation. Despite this, the budget wouldn't stretch to two full time players. In fact, we didn't really *have* a budget.

We decided to compromise. We already knew of Paul, a good standard New Zealander in the area, who could play at least the first few games before returning home, and decided that we would supplement him with one full-time, paid, real American. We brought over a 6ft 8in forward called Dan O'Neil, fresh from the University of Hawaii.

There were two problems with this approach. First, Paul's spell in the UK proved shorter than anyone thought. He was a good player – I think that he went on to represent his country – but was on his way back by mid October. Oh yes, and New Zealand were ranked about 85th in the world. Second, Uxbridge was not Hawaii. Had we followed the examples of Halifax and Bradford, and promoted Uxbridge as a tourist destination, we might have hidden this. But there were no flies on Dan. It took him 10 days to spot the difference, but once he did, he was off.

*   *   *

Our first two league games were against the same team, the newly restyled West Bromwich Kestrels. In marked contrast to Brunel, the Kestrels seemed just the sort of team that the league wanted to attract. They had assumed the franchise previously occupied by Wolverhampton, had an inner city catchment area, and were working on self sufficiency through the establishment of a private members drinking club. Our record quickly had a familiar look about it – Played Two, Lost Two.

That, though, was only part of the story. Encouraged by the impact made in our first home game of the previous season, we decided to put a premium price on this year's equivalent sponsorship. Endsleigh Insurance agreed to take a later game, probably reasoning that there were enough of last year's leaflets still washing about the campus for the moment.

The commercial know how to exploit this opportunity came from Chairman Mike. Other club chairmen rubbed shoulders with the elite of British society.

Ours knew the manager of our local bank. And not just any bank. Barclays Bank. Barclays was the only bank that had spent much of the past decade being subject to a student boycott.

Throughout the 1970s, the attention of student unions, along with all right minded people, had turned to the evil apartheid regime in South Africa. Sanctions were regarded as a practical way of promoting change, and attention was turned on those British companies that continued to defy logic and invest in the regime. Throughout the 1970s, Barclays had been seen as a prime target. By 1982 the boycott was over, although whether this reflected an improved attitude on the part of the bank, or recognition that they were just one of many offenders was not clear. It was obvious, however, that some people on campus still bore a grudge.

Our jovial, rugby playing and beer swilling chairman seemed oblivious to this background. And when Graham, the newly elected student union officer responsible for clubs and societies, and I raised the issue, he was unrepentant.

'Mike – how could you possibly *not* know about Barclays?' I exploded.

'Well, nobody who comes in here ever complains about it.'

'That's because you're a right wing bigot who never leaves the Sports Centre.'

'Hang on a minute,' interrupted Graham. 'I think he's got a point'.

Mike and I looked around in eager anticipation. Graham was a Chemist. He was not noted for his political skills.

'Well, what Mike's saying is that no one who comes into the Sports Centre gives a fig about Barclays.'

'Apart from me, yes…'

'And what you're saying is that most politicos don't give a fig about sport.'

'Well, yes. Apart from me. So?'

'So – all we have to do is keep them apart. You're the only person who would notice.'

Surely the whole purpose of sponsorship was publicity. How could you possibly have a sponsored game, and hide the fact from half the campus? On the other hand, why should Barclays care if people who are not going to bank with them on principle don't know that they are sponsoring the game? And how could people who objected to Barclays being on campus be offended, if they didn't know about it?

A complicated plan evolved, at first frivolously, but with increasing seriousness. Until a day before the match, we would put up normal posters only, with a blank bit in the sponsor's section. From Friday, the Barclays logo would emerge, at first in the Sports Centre, but then with increasing boldness to the rest of the campus, leading to a crescendo as the bus for an anti something demonstration pulled away from the campus on Saturday morning. By Saturday evening, the court would be decked out with Barclays material. Even the programmes could be fitted in to the plan, since Barclays had offered to print their own covers, to be collated by hand. Of course the Print Room, its last year of student union management, might have smelled a rat, but they thought nothing of being asked to print posters with an empty blur in the middle and programmes without covers. They printed stuff of similar quality week in, week out.

Amazingly, the plan worked, if not quite to perfection, well enough to achieve our objective of securing the sponsorship without protest. We even managed to get most of the posters removed before the demonstration coach returned. Combined with all this, the game itself seemed almost incidental.

*   *   *

The first two games showed promise, but the fact remained that promotion was already slipping out of our grasp, and our all time National League record stood at a miserable seven wins and 25 defeats. Worse still, six of the seven wins were against just three teams, and one of those no longer existed.

Something had to be done. 1981 was, after all, the year of action, and the obvious course of action was to recruit a second American. Coach Tony had already replaced Dan, our American from Hawaii, with Bob, an American from France – or at least that's where he had played the previous season. That seemed much safer. Now, out of the blue we were offered the services of one Dave Anderson, formerly of Xavier University, Ohio, more recently of Brighton, England and most recently of all unemployed, but well regarded, in the country and affordable. In the spirit of 1981, we went for it.

Perhaps it is my imagination, or perhaps we were already getting used to disappointment in our American signings, but the introduction of Bob and Dave to the fans, in the match programme for next home game against Bradford, seems a bit muted. Dave, it pointed out, had been 'made available' by Brighton. He was in his first season in England, was reputed to be a very mobile player (as, of course, had been Dan), and an excellent dunker who should keep the crowd entertained. We were even vaguer about Bob. He had played in France last season and was 'settling in well'.

What we didn't say was whether either was any good. The main reason was that we didn't know – or at least I didn't. We had managed to send Coach Tony as far as Brighton on a scouting mission, but didn't have the resources to view players in America, or pay fees to agents. In the absence of such luxuries, there were lots of theories about how to recruit. Bradford had gone for brains – both of their Americans came from Harvard. An alternative theory was that players who had graduated in Business were a good bet, because they were more likely to have gone to college purely for their basketball ability – unlike their peers who had been able to master complicated subjects like science. We were not the only people to realise this dilemma. Hence the story of the American college coach, considering a student for a basketball scholarship, who asked for an academic reference. The answer came back that 'this student produces straight A's, but his B's are still a little wobbly.'

Bob and Dave had both graduated in business, but neither was stupid, and both *were* good at basketball. In fact, it took us a while to find out exactly how good they were. At first, the combination didn't look as though it would set the league alight. Certainly it didn't provide the dominance that second division teams expected of their Americans. In the Bradford game, the pair contributed just two baskets each in the first 18 minutes, and a combined total of only 28 points.

It was a case of glass half empty, or glass half full? Had we signed two ordinary Americans whose contribution was going to be way below that of their compatriots at other clubs? Or did we have greater depth in English players and, better still, a pair of Americans who were willing to play as a team?

*   *   *

Then something weird happened. I mean something *really* weird. We started to win. I'm not talking about winning the odd game. I mean game after game after game. It was so weird, for a team that had previously won only seven games in over two seasons, that it took us some time to realise what was happening.

Colchester was next up after the Bradford game. They were one of our bankers from the start of the season, so a win – even a comfortable one – seemed nothing special. Next, we travelled to Bolton. They were a new team in the league, so we didn't know what to expect, but a four point win seemed acceptable. Then we played Camden and Nottingham – both among the select few teams that we had beaten in the past. Then it was the return game against Bolton, who of course we had just beaten, so we kind of expected to do so again. Then, on the Saturday before Christmas, a first ever visit to the latest incarnation of Milton Keynes, also in the lower reaches of the league. Another win was expected, and duly arrived. With seven wins and two defeats, we were third in the league table. In less than two months, the Brunel Ducks had doubled their tally of wins for the previous two seasons.

None of the results were remarkable individually, but collectively their impact was huge. Coming back from the Bolton game, pretending to be asleep, I overheard players and Coach Tony discussing how long it would be before they would be able to turn full-time. Having my lunch in the student bar on the day after the return against Bolton, I listened with incredulity to another discussion between two students who were debating whether our recovery from a 13 point deficit to win was fixed – 'like the wrestling'. The point was, though, that people were talking about us. The Sports Centre laid on an additional basketball session on Friday afternoons, normally a dead period when engineering students were still frantically studying and social scientists had already arrived home for the weekend. Within a year, Brunel had its third men's team, and two women's teams.

We stepped up off campus publicity, too. Some organisations would have bought advertising space. We thought this too conventional and too expensive. Our alternative approach included a regular Sunday lunchtime delivery of match posters to local pubs. Do you know how many pubs there are within three miles of the Brunel campus? Well, in 1982 there were 39, and getting to them all in Carol's mini, getting the posters in and agreement that someone would put them up was quite a challenge. This was all the more so since it had to be done in an hour. Pubs opened at 12, and we reckoned that after one o'clock they would be too full, and it would take too long to get to talk to the barman. Added to which, an hour of popping in and out of pubs without having a drink was too much for anyone.

*   *   *

Having at last recruited two high quality, stable and reasonably affordable full-time players, we needed a strategy to keep them. Further economic incentives were naturally out of the question, so we concluded that the best approach would be to get them into long term relationships with English partners. This might seem ambitious, even intrusive, but we were quite serious. We even had a committee meeting about it – and don't think that we were the only club to consider the possibility.

'Someone on the campus would be ideal', was one view.

'Mmm. We'd save on accommodation then, too.

'A first year would be best – she'd be here for another three years.'

'The marrying kind – obviously. He could be a dual national by the time she left.'

'And someone who doesn't want to move to the States. That would be a disaster!'

It was an optimistic policy, and a risky one. The female population at Brunel was as attractive as at any other university – but nowhere near as numerous. Ian was already going out with one of the most eligible candidates in the student population, although at least he had the decency to bring her with him, and Phil was quickly going out with her best friend. Any further reduction of the supply of available girls at the hands of basketball stars could lead to a revolt among our male market. The ideal profile of a first year – aged perhaps 18 or 19 – seemed a bit young. Moreover, Coach Tony would probably have something to say about the saving on accommodation costs. Brunel study bedrooms were not designed for two, especially when the second was over 6ft tall. Ian was always complaining about it.

We decided to broaden our horizons beyond the campus, and Will was deputed to identify suitable opportunities for socialising. He was well qualified for the role, and pursued it with enthusiasm, but to no avail. There was not a whiff of a marriage during the remaining six years. Not even the prospect of a little dual national to who we could look to lead the team in 20 years time. It was all a huge disappointment.

*   *   *

For the first time in my life, I was involved in something fashionable, and it wasn't a comfortable feeling. I was not used to it, and had a distinct feeling that it wouldn't last. A glance at the fixture list heightened the fear – two out of our three games in January were against the runaway league leaders Leicester. We lost them both, together with a close away game at Bradford. By the end of January, our record was a more realistic Won seven, Lost five.

I was right to think that the winning run couldn't continue, but wrong to think that a few defeats would upset the momentum. For a start, the manner of the defeats wasn't as bad as I had feared. The home game against Leicester produced the only occasion in the whole season when they looked like losing – we were 11 points up at half-time and still level going into the last five minutes. No one was disappointed at the entertainment levels among the record crowd of over 500, who presumably were still discussing the experience the following lunchtime in their 39 different pubs.

We won our remaining four league games comfortably, leaving us with 11 wins and third place, but we pass over this quickly. The real highlight of early 1982 came in an obscure competition called the National Trophy.

*   *   *

As its name suggests, the National Trophy was open to any team in England. Except, that is, the ones who were any good – or at any rate good enough to be in the first division. In football terms, it was a cross between the Full Members Cup and the Freight Rover Trophy. If you have never heard of either competition, you can draw your own conclusions. Entry wasn't confined to Division Two teams, but not many others entered. This particular year Watford (Royals) had done so, as part of their campaign to stress their national league credentials, and had been rewarded for their enterprise with defeat by over 100 points at Leicester in the first round.

I have not mentioned the National Trophy before, because there was no reason to. Certainly we had never won a match in it. This particular year, it assumed a new importance. Our chances of promotion had almost disappeared before our run of good form had got under way, so the Trophy gave us an opportunity to show what might have been. The first round produced a comfortable win against Camden, the quarter-final produced an opportunity to win at Bradford – the only team outside the top two to beat us in the league. That set up the semi-final that we had wanted all along – at home to the West Bromwich Kestrels.

West Brom had deserved their two victories over us in September and October, but we were under strength on both occasions and had not got used to playing together as a team. How much had we improved? We would certainly get the chance to find out. The Kestrels team included nine of the 10 players who had visited Brunel in the previous October.

We expected a more even game, and we got one. We led for the entire first half, but contrived to be one point behind at the interval. The lead changed hands 10 times in the next 10 minutes, but then the Kestrels established a narrow lead. Ian tied the scores at 89 all with less than four minutes to go. And then…

Well, then Bob and Dave produced 13 points without reply. It was probably the most triumphant three minutes of basketball yet seen at Brunel, and the crowd loved it – 600 odd of them. My mind quickly turned to how many we could expect for the final, inevitably against Leicester, but also at Brunel. Come to think of it, how many could we fit in?

*   *   *

There were two ways of working out a crowd limit. The first was to ask the university safety officer – a nice chap, but rather too serious for my taste. The second was to look for a precedent that could be used to justify packing the place to the rafters. Today, I would do the first without hesitation. In the 1980s that option seemed boring, bureaucratic and, if it produced the wrong answer, very costly.

I could think of two previous occasions when a thousand or so people had packed into the Sports Centre. The first was a concert from the *Sex Pistols*, probably in about 1977, and certainly at the height of their notoriety. Such an event *must* have been less safe than any scenario likely to arise from a basketball match, but was difficult to cite for two reasons. Although the night had attained almost legendary status, no one knew anybody who would admit actually having been there. I for one had locked myself in my room for the whole night. Also, even the organisers didn't know how many people had attended in the end, because the evening had been one of near complete anarchy.

The second example was a mass meeting of students, also in late 1977. Normally, student union meetings could be housed in an average sized telephone box, let alone a full sized sports hall, but this one was different. A few weeks earlier, student activists had occupied the University Council Chamber in protest against something. This was not a rare occurrence, nor did it present a major threat. Day to day use of the Council Chamber was hardly critical to the smooth operation of the university. Some would say that its main uses – meetings of the University Council and Senate – were actually detrimental. This university, however, regarded the occupation of its property as a matter of principle. It decreed that, if a student meeting did not order the end of the occupation, the university would be closed, lock stock and barrel, until common sense prevailed.

This strategy had a fatal flaw. The ultimatum was issued just two weeks before the end of Christmas term, with no examinations in sight. To the average student, the decision was a no brainer. Throughout 1977 and 1978, Jim Callaghan had been able to maintain a minority government because, in his own words, for the smaller parties to bring him down would be 'like turkeys voting for Christmas'. Well, turkeys may not vote for Christmas, but Brunel students certainly did. The meeting had been packed, with a majority voting to continue the occupation, or rather, to extend the holidays. The vote was promptly reversed in January, but it had two major implications. It earned Brunel a place in history among the select few British universities to be closed due to student militancy. And it provided us with a precedent to demonstrate that the Sports Centre could accommodate over 900 people.

You could argue that, while the thousand or so who had attended the student union meeting had the whole hall to fit into, we by contrast had to accommodate the small matter of a basketball match in the middle. But as we have already observed, this was a time for action rather than undue attention to detail. Armed with this evidence, we proceeded to print, and sell, 900 tickets. The night went absolutely according to expectations – including, unfortunately, the game itself. There was never the remotest possibility of an upset, and Leicester ran out winners by 94–78. But the atmosphere was fantastic – a real indication of the potential for basketball on the campus, and how far the club had come during the season. The way we saw things, Leicester had been the best team in the league by a mile, but next season there would be no Leicester to worry about, and we were next in line.

*   *   *

In the wider world of basketball, the rise of the Brunel Ducks went almost unnoticed, dwarfed by a tide of national events that promised to change the game forever.

Basketball was growing fast. In 1972 the newly established English Basketball League had just six members. Finals of the National Championship, a knock out competition dating back to 1936, had been staged in venues as diverse as the Royal Albert Hall and South Ruislip Leisure Centre, but received little attention. There were no full time players, and virtually no external sponsorship. Yet by 1980, the National League had expanded to two men's divisions, junior and women's divisions were fully operational, the National Championships had been established over two days at Wembley Area, and the knock out National Cup as a separate competition, with its own final. Both the Championship and Cup finals received national television time. Media coverage and attendances had soared.

The English Basket Ball Association, which only appointed its first full-time administrator in 1970, successfully encouraged this expansion. Increasingly, however, growth depended on the ambition and investment of individual clubs. As the sport developed, it became clear that the interests of clubs and the national association were not the same.

The EBBA and leading clubs were united in the ability to think – or at least talk – big. They proudly reported the results of a survey showing that basketball was now, 'Britain's fastest growing team sport', and predicted that the upwards trend was set to continue. It became a marketing slogan for years to come.

'Britain's fastest growing team sport'. What *exactly*, did that mean? Anyone with half a brain would realise that it didn't say much about how many people actually played, watched or otherwise followed basketball. It merely meant that it was proportionately more than in previous years. More than highlighting a widespread surge in popularity, it reflected the low base from which English basketball had started. In statistical terms, it was a claim that could equally be true of a recently invented sport that had attracted its first 10 participants.

The statistics, though, were convenient. They seemed to confirm the belief of all involved that the world was changing, and in ways that supported our cause. The public of the 1980s wanted to watch sport at a time and a location that suited them, in clean, warm conditions and an environment to which they could take their family, or which offered the opportunity of a night out. Football, which we arrogantly considered to be our major rival, was suffering on all of these counts. Loss making clubs had not invested in facilities, insisted on playing their matches at three o'clock on Saturday afternoons and offered nothing by way of post-match entertainment. Worst of all, football was struggling to free itself from the violence and hooliganism that had beset it during the 1970s. Attendances were plummeting. In 1981–82 they declined to 20 million, by far the lowest since World War Two, and a reduction of almost two million on the previous low a season before. In two years, league football had lost almost 20 per cent of its audience, and there were further reductions to come.

The media was changing, too. After 17 years of being restricted to three national television channels, 1982 was to see the launch of a fourth. The imaginatively named Channel Four had a brief to widen the viewing experience of the public, and sport would not be exempt from this. Rumours were rife that Basketball was a major part of their plans.

*   *   *

Excitement reached fever pitch in January 1982, when the *Daily Mail* broke a story that the basketball authorities were negotiating a deal worth up to £2 million for marketing rights. The rights would be sold centrally, with the international sports marketing firm West Nally taking the lead. A critical element in the arrangement would be the guarantee of national television time. This would come from a two-year deal for regular Monday night basketball, now in the final stages of negotiation with Channel Four.

Within months, the Channel Four deal had been signed – it was indeed a two-year arrangement that involved 19 live matches during the first season, to be shown on Monday nights, climaxing in full coverage of the Championship final from Wembley in March. The riches from marketing seemed certain to follow, although the format of these was less certain. Presented with plans that would generate some £40,000 for each Division One club per season, some clubs felt that they could do better alone, and were reluctant to sign up unless compensated for this.

Nevertheless, the idea of central marketing appeared to have been agreed in principle. EBBA representative officer Peter Sprogis confirmed in *Basketball Monthly* that, 'it is the clubs intention to operate together under a group marketing concept, with or without West Nally as consultants'. The company ultimately established to facilitate this, Basketball Marketing Limited, allowed clubs more freedom to secure key sponsorships individually, although Sprogis still insisted that there would be 'exclusive contracts for items such as boots, strip and basketballs, and clubs will need approval before selling courtside advertising'.

Basketball Marketing Limited was based on an assumption that the *product* – in this case top class basketball – was more important than any individual club. This was a big mistake. Eliminating inequality was critical to producing more close games and uncertainty of outcome, but the few clubs with access to money first and foremost wanted to win, and were reluctant to give up their financial advantage for any wider benefit to the sport. It was a problem prophetically seen by an editorial in *Basketball Monthly*:

'Before the fine print of any agreement can be inked in, the clubs must agree on more fundamental questions of group philosophy. Are the clubs really ready to restrict their competitive instincts to the court? Are they really ready to pull together, or was it only the promise of a substantial cash share out which fostered sudden camaraderie?…What would happen if the financial guarantees did disappear? Which clubs would want to pull together? If they did not make known their feelings very quickly we would soon find out the clubs who were determined to go it alone again, as they always have done in the past. And if there were no cash guarantees, which clubs would disappear altogether, having been sustained only by the promise of a pot of gold at the end of basketball's rainbow.'

Basketball Marketing Limited was not about the marketing of basketball as such, but the 12 clubs that made up the National Division One. Soon after the negotiations had been made public, the first division clubs made it clear that

Division Two clubs – not to mention the junior and women's areas of the game – would be excluded from any benefits.

These arguments have since become familiar to any follower of soccer, rugby league, or rugby union. Starting from the reasonable premise that it is the top level of the sport that is most saleable to television, and therefore sponsors, they extend to the notion that, to maintain that level, it is the top clubs that need the continuity. This in turn requires investment, and if owners are expected to produce this investment, then this too needs to be protected. This in turn requires that their place at the top level should be secure. Not only, therefore, should the clubs in the top division receive all the revenue, but they should be freed from the prospect of relegation. If there is no relegation, then there cannot be any promotion, unless the league is to expand – and significant expansion is not desirable since it would dilute the share of revenue for each club.

For much of the 1981–82 season, it was unclear whether any promotion would take place at all. When it was eventually agreed that Leicester should be allowed in, the top clubs sought to preserve their 'one 12th' share by excluding Manchester, only to be overruled by intervention from the game's National Executive Committee. In the years that followed, the future of promotion and relegation would be a constant battle.

*   *   *

At Brunel, our expenditure for 1981–82 had been under £10,000. The thought that clubs had rejected a central allocation of over four times that amount seemed astonishing. The fact that absolutely no part of the windfall should go beyond the small number of First Division clubs seemed outrageous. On the other hand, the thought struck us that we were on the verge of the First Division ourselves. The same thought evidently struck a few people from outside the club, too.

A call arrived from Will, who had been approached by Coach Tony, who had been approached by a consortium, who wanted to meet with the Directors. Most of us had never spoken to a consortium in our lives. Some of us didn't even know what a consortium was. The curiosity was too much.

We didn't know much about this particular consortium, either, because it wished to remain anonymous. Their representative was a youngish chap, who

Tony knew and assured us was both credible and a genuinely interested in basketball. He worked in the electronics industry. He boosted his credentials by telling us that he travelled widely in the Far East on business, then ruined them by telling us that mobile phones were going to be the next huge market. As if *anyone* was going to believe that!

Justin (not his real name, but anonymity was the order of the day) explained that he represented a consortium of 'high value' individuals. They had seen the potential of basketball, and thought that the Ducks would be an ideal vehicle through which to exploit the opportunity. It was a unique opportunity to take the club forward.

The only thing was that these were *business* people. This point was constantly emphasised; perhaps reflecting a fear that a group of people who didn't understand the concept of a consortium didn't understand that of business either. *Business* people, it appeared, would need a *return* on their *investment* – a *financial* return. They still loved basketball, but their time was precious. This was, after all, the 1980s.

Having explained the basic premises of capitalism, Justin invited us to ask questions. So we did.

'Could you tell us more about the individuals concerned?'

'No. They are high profile people, so they need to keep a low profile.'

'How much money have they got, and what will they pay for the club?'

'(a) Lots. (b) Nothing. Their main contribution would be business expertise.'

'So they don't actually want to *run* the club?'

'Of course not. These are busy people! But, well, they are also *business people*. And *business* people need to have *tangible assets*.

'So they want to *own* the club?'

'Oh, we could negotiate that. As long as they own the holding company.'

'So, what would the holding company do?'

'Well, that would own the club.'

'And they think that Brunel is a good base for the investment?'

'Yes, they know that Brunel is the current base.'

'Wouldn't it continue as the base then?'

'Well, that would be a business decision. You can't expect *business* people to make decisions on *non-business* grounds.'

'But we'd be part of that decision, right?'

'Oh yes, your advice would be vital to the holding company.'

'But the holding company would be owned by...?

'The consortium.'

Our excitement stared to wane. However much we probed and prodded, the basic facts were that a group of unnamed individuals wanted to take over the effective running of the club, were not prepared to tell us very much about what they would do with it or how much they would invest, and certainly didn't plan to pay anything up front. It wasn't that we had an inflated value of our own worth (in fact, our main source of suspicion was how the consortium expected to secure their return). It wasn't that we didn't trust the consortium (we didn't even know who they were). It was just that there was nothing on which to base those decisions.

It was all a great disappointment to Tony, who had made the introduction for the best of reasons, and rightly concluded that the current hotch potch of a committee were unlikely to produce the playing budget that he needed. For once, though, the rest of the group were solid. Maybe we thought that a better offer might come along. Maybe we were just stubborn. Maybe, unlikely though it sounds against the backdrop of the 1980s, we had principles. Ultimately, it didn't really matter very much, because no one was actually offering to buy. For better or worse, we were going to face the brave new world of basketball alone.

PROPHETS WITHOUT PROFITS

As 1982 began, Bucks Fizz were top of the charts with *Land of Make Believe*. In April, Imagination had a hit with *It's an Illusion*. They were followed in May by the unlikely promises of the England World Cup team, that *This Time* things would be different, and of their Scottish counterparts that they *Have a Dream*. Come June, both were eliminated from the tournament almost before it had begun.

We might have taken the hint that society, basketball and the Brunel Ducks in particular were entering a period of bloated expectations, and that caution should be the order of the day. We didn't. Instead, we succumbed to the dilemma exposed by the commentator Adrian Childs in describing the problems of supporting West Bromwich Albion Football Club. 'Disappointment', he reflected, was not the problem, it was the 'hope and expectation' preceding it that was so difficult to cope with.

Hope and expectation were big problems for the Ducks in the summer of 1982. The facts, as we saw them, were these. Basketball was taking off in a big way. Where television went, the fans, sponsorship and money would follow. And we were there – well, almost. We were just one division away from the big time, and one of the two best teams in our division. This was a unique opportunity. We needed to keep our nerve and invest.

And, of course, this was the 1980s. It was a decade in which, if you believed our political leaders, making money was not only possible and respectable, but the nearest thing anyone had to a social obligation. All it needed was a good idea, hard work, and a bare minimum of talent. We had at least two of the three attributes, so we reckoned that we fitted bill well.

With all the experience of a 21-year-old, I had not thought that Margaret Thatcher would make much difference when she came to power in 1979. I was surprised how alarmed people were at her election. I remember arguing with anyone who would listen that there was no reason for undue depression.

Elections, I explained, came and went. The only other Conservative government that I could remember hadn't had much impact – short of leaving the country on a three-day week and running short of fuel. I imagined that Margaret Thatcher would be much the same.

History confirms that I was wrong. Whether Margaret Thatcher changed much about the way we lived is debatable, but she certainly changed the way in which we thought. Unlike the Callaghan administration, which according to legend had forced people to hide their money under the bed with a top rate of taxation of 98 per cent, the Thatcher government told us to make money, and to flaunt it to the extent of arrogance.

This advice could have been written for the world of basketball – particularly the bit about arrogance. Almost everyone – from the typical programme seller and supporters club secretary to the lady who did the refreshments – was posing as a small (or even large) businessman. All were looking to make a few quid, all carried briefcases. All displayed the language, if not the brains, of the new market economy. All, it seemed, ignored the fact that the money was simply not there to be made.

*   *   *

These were times for bold decisions, and we made them in abundance. Our budget increased to the dizzy heights of £14,000 – just short of the transfer fee that Solent had paid two seasons earlier for a single player. In the best traditions of basketball, well over half of this was devoted to our two American stars, whose salaries were almost twice that of their predecessors, and, of course, infinitely higher than those of Mike and Vaughan two years previously.

This time, we reasoned, we had reduced the risk. Our star signing was Larry McKinney, ex-first round draft with the Indiana Pacers in the NBA, who had played for most of the previous season with Team Talbot in the English First Division, where his average of over 30 points per game persuaded *Basketball Monthly* that he would be one of the Division's most valuable players. Alongside him was Larry Sheldon – shorter, at a mere 6 foot 5 inches, built like an American footballer, and as mild a mannered guy as you could hope to meet, with the exception, perhaps, of the 40 minutes that he spent on a basketball court every Saturday night – although we were yet to learn this.

There was change, too, among the English players. Nigel had been conscripted to take part in the latest phase of the war between Hemel and Watford, and there was no Bob Senior or Bob Spencer. On the other hand we recruited Mike Short, initially from the area, who had returned after studying in Leeds, Dave Yewman and Neil Clark, who had not played in the National League before but had graduated from Crystal Palace juniors. We reckoned that we had just about broken even.

We sat back and waited for the good times – but they never quite arrived. It's hard for someone with as little technical knowledge of basketball as I to judge what actually went wrong. Both Larrys were really nice guys, clean living (by the standards of basketball) and got on with each other well enough to share a house and (loaned) car. Perhaps they were too committed, and used to playing at a higher level. Perhaps our expectations were just too high. Whatever – frustration set in from the word go.

The fixture list did us no favours. For the second year in a row our first two league games were against the same club – in this case a rejuvenated Bolton, who turned out to be one of the strongest in the league. Added to which Team Talbot and the league had failed to mention that Larry M was carrying over a one match suspension from the previous season, and would therefore miss the first game. We should, of course, have checked ourselves, but even had we done so, such was our confidence that this was the right signing that we would probably have gone ahead anyway.

After two games, the season already seemed to be in ruins. Basketball does not have the same element of uncertainty as football. As Leicester had proved the previous year, it was quite possible for a team to finish the season unbeaten. To lose two games, in a season in which only one team, at best, was likely to win promotion, was a disaster. Worse still, we lost them to a team that we didn't even know *were* promotion rivals. Most people assumed that West Bromwich and Brunel, having finished second and third in the previous seasons, would be the main contenders.

*   *   *

Such was our sense of disappointment, that the small matter of breaking the record for the biggest win in the history of the league went almost unnoticed.

Our programme notes stressed that Milton Keynes would be tough opponents, but the group that emerged from their mini bus looked more like Snow White and the seven dwarfs. In a traumatic six weeks they had replaced two Americans, a dual national and a string of experienced English players with just one new signing – a seven foot plus local with little or no experience, who they had spotted in a local shopping centre. They had also evolved a whole new concept in tactics, in which the dwarfs threw the ball as high as possible, without much regard for direction, in the hope that the seven foot tall Snow White would catch it. The approach was doomed to failure, especially when Snow White fouled out, and the final margin of 88 points fully reflected the game. I almost began to sympathise with Solent, who had edged past us by a mere 71 points three years earlier. At least we didn't have to do this every week.

*   *   *

Another diversion came with the arrival of Channel Four on 7 November. The new venture could hardly have made a better start. The first programme ever to be broadcast was *Countdown*, a mildly intellectual quiz show which went on to become a staple part of the late afternoon diet for pensioners, housewives and student layabouts the length and breadth of the country. It was still going strong almost 30 years later.

There was no reason to think that basketball would be any less successful. Channel Four had decided to focus on two sports only – the other being American football. Basketball, we reasoned, had most potential because the games would be British. For once, the game pulled together in promoting the televised matches. The first game could not have been better. Crystal Palace beat Birmingham thanks to a basket just seven seconds from time from a young English star, Trevor Anderson. The following day, we were assured by *Basketball Monthly*, every child in the playground wanted to be Trevor Anderson. Unfortunately not enough playgrounds had basketball stands for the would-be Trevors to shoot at.

By week three, the euphoria was fading. Some blamed Channel Four production techniques. Others pointed to the Monday night scheduling, or the choice of match. Only the second half was covered live, and in too many cases the result was a foregone conclusion even before this started. American football, played between teams that people had heard of, and leading up to Super Bowl, proved a bigger rival than we had expected. Nor was Channel Four the only new television phenomenon in town. Early 1984 would see the launch of TV AM. Basketball had enough problems in coping with American Football as a rival. It was certainly no match for Roland Rat.

*   *   *

It was becoming clear that we could not rely on Channel Four for our media needs, so we started to look elsewhere. The Division One clubs still harboured hopes that the BBC, which had covered an annual international tournament at Crystal Palace for several years, would develop an interest in regular league games. We were more modest in our aspirations. We focussed on Radio Hillingdon Hospital.

The addition of Radio Hillingdon Hospital to our media portfolio meant that we could now boast regular coverage on *two* radio stations – the other being the campus based *Radio Brunel.* As with all media relations, this required careful negotiation. I eventually agreed a package with an ambitious young reporter called Bob, involving a free press pass, free match programme and free place on the coach to selected away games. It was expensive, but we were in the big time now, and you had to invest to accumulate.

Fleetingly, I wondered whether hospital radio would have quite the same age profile as that of a university based basketball team, or indeed whether it had any listeners at all. I even wondered whether it was *safe* for those with vulnerable health to be subject to our match commentaries. But all of these considerations paled into insignificance compared with the boost to our image. Henceforth, we would have a *real* journalist on our bus to away games, with a *real* tape recorder to conduct interviews. Who cared if anyone was listening?

It was another small step on the road to national prominence – not only for us, but for our aspiring reporter, Bob Ballard. I'm reminded of this even today, when I hear him on *BBC Radio Five* summarising premiership football, swimming and gymnastics from all over the world. I wonder whether he still gets a free place in the competitor's bus?

* * *

By mid December, our record comprised six wins and four losses. In previous seasons, we would have been delighted with this; now it seemed like a disaster. We had already lost too many games to reach the 'promised land', and the money was running out fast. Like the Israelites, we began to doubt whether the 'promised land' really existed. Unlike the Israelites, we had no free manna from heaven to tide us over.

Our next game, at home to league newcomers Gateshead, was expected to add to the wins tally. The first half, however, seemed to be a microcosm of the entire season. We threatened to establish a lead, but never quite made it, and by half-time had slipped back to a seven point deficit. There were more false dawns in the second half, but by the ninth minute the gap had slipped further to 13 when, to make things worse Larry M got into an altercation with a Gateshead player. Both were dismissed.

The effect was hardly equal. Larry M was 6ft 11in and American, his opponent 5ft 10in and English. To add insult to injury, Larry's frustration boiled over on his way out from the court, punching the door so hard that his fist went clean through a glass panel. It wasn't going to be our night, and there was worse to come.

For a while, Larry S and the English squad seemed capable of making an unlikely recovery. Within four minutes, the deficit was down to six. Larry was playing out of his skin. Those who knew him though, could see that all was not well. One of the quietest, friendliest and most courteous people you could ever meet, Larry seemed to acquire a completely different character the moment that he stepped onto a basketball court. Worst of all, Larry had a real sense of injustice, and the sense was becoming stronger and stronger with every decision that went against us. On the night in question, this seemed to be most of them.

Four minutes from time, things were getting desperate. Larry launched a drive to the basket, through a seemingly impossible space. The ball went through the basket, two Gateshead players went flying, and Larry kept running. The referee was perfectly placed behind the basket and decided that the defenders had been stationery, and that the foul was Larry's. Larry didn't agree, and expressed his view in the clearest way possible. He just kept on running. Nothing was going to stop him – especially not the referee, who was directly in his flight path.

A collision with a well built, 6ft 5in basketball player still running at full speed, is no joke. A few seconds later, the referee was falling uncontrollably backwards, remarkably staying on his feet for 20ft or so before colliding with the climbing wall at the back of the gym. The crowd loved it. Most thought it the highlight of a very bad night. The referee took a different view. Larry S became our second American star to be dismissed, and the game petered out to a miserable conclusion.

We knew that the matter wouldn't end there. Dismissals were serious matters, usually involving suspensions. Two in one game was very bad news, especially when they were your star players and the second offence had all the characteristics of a mugging. No one was more aware of this than Larry S. At a time when the only sensible course of action was to go home and calm down, Larry reverted to his more normal, nice guy, role. He wanted to explain himself right way, and the direct approach was the only one that he knew. He went and hammered on the door of the referees changing rooms.

Understandably, the referees did not immediately assume that the thudding noise on their door was part of a peace keeping mission. They called the match Commissioner, asking for protection. Now, at last, we were going to find out what Commissioners did.

*　　*　　*

Well before football discovered that it needed a fourth official to hold a board up at the end of each half, or cricket discovered the need for a third umpire to watch television all day, a fourth umpire to turn the sound up and a referee to make sure that he did it properly, basketball invented the concept of the Commissioner. Unlike the other sports, there were no circumstances in which the Commissioner would replace the referee – most were past retirement age. Commissioners existed to resolve 'off court' disputes and, ominously, to report back on the whole occasion to the English Basket Ball Association.

Generally speaking, I didn't like Commissioners – they were just another expense and I took the view that people should pay us to watch our games, rather than the other way round. However this opinion was gradually changing. The EBBA had recently negotiated a clause in the league sponsorship with drinks producers *Just Juice*, providing for a bonus of £30 every time a team attracted a crowd of 350 or more. Commissioners were responsible for reporting crowd figures back to the EBBA, so they were worth buttering up a bit, particularly as attendances dipped towards the end of the season. Our last four crowds of 1982–83 were officially reported as 362, 354, 359 and, with increasing boldness, 375. Thirty pounds was £30.

The exceptions to this rule were local Commissioners, who were both sympathetic and didn't cost much. Harry was a prime example of this. Not only had he only travelled from central London, but he had done so on the tube, and regularly waived his match fee. Harry was a true gent. Long since retired, he had a distinguished war record of which he hardly ever spoke, and talked with much more passion of his profession as a tailor than the woes of basketball. I liked Harry.

Half an hour after the game, when all good Commissioners should be focussing on the quality of the post-match refreshments, Harry was a popular man. The referees wanted protection. The crowd wanted the referees. Mike wanted to know who was responsible for his broken glass door, and I wanted to confirm that the attendance was 426 – even if most had left before the end. Larry S wanted to explain himself to anyone who would listen. Faced with these urgent and conflicting demands, Harry gave the wisest judgement I had heard in my basketball career to date.

'I've just remembered', he declared, 'that I have locked my sister out of our flat. I have to go now.'

And, as an afterthought, 'but do send a copy of your match video to Leeds. I think they'll be interested'.

And off he went. That was the end of the complaints for the evening, because there was no one left to complain to. Had it not been for the afterthought, it would have been the perfect judgement. Why, oh why, did we have a match video? It was just about the one thing that the league rules *didn't* require us to have.

On the other hand it was, as Harry had inadvertently pointed out, *our* video, and it was very much going to stay that way. Our video producer Niall displayed amazing professional pride, for someone who did not get paid, but to no avail. Once the officials had been removed, so was the video. We would blame the equipment if at all possible, but if we had to fall back on human error, Niall being suspended was not a disaster. If an EBBA disciplinary panel saw the video, then the penalty dished out to Larry Sheldon might well be. By the time the authorities asked for the video on the following Monday, it had disappeared.

Even the English Basket Ball Association was not stupid enough to believe that the absence of a video meant that there was no case to answer. It did, though, give us the chance to tell our side of the story, unencumbered by the facts. The question was – what exactly *was* our side of the story? Dismissals were normally punished with a suspension, and frustration did not qualify as an excuse.

Suspensions or not, we could not afford to keep two full-time Americans at the rates we were paying them. We would have to face this issue at some point, and the dismissals forced our hand. It was two weeks before Christmas, and there were no games (and no revenue) for two weeks over the holiday period. It was quite possible that the suspended players would not play again until February, and the season would be over in mid-March.

We calculated that we could afford to keep one Larry, but not both. We now had no chance of promotion, but there were coaching commitments in schools to honour, and it was important to keep attendances and morale up. The problem was that, on the basis of performances to date, the Larry to retain was Larry S, and on the nature of the offences it was Larry S who was likely to get the longest suspension.

We reckoned that the EBBA had bigger fish to fry than us, particularly given our reputation for arguing endlessly and the fact that, with no video, the decision would come down to personal accounts. Our strategy would be to determine the punishment that we wanted to see in place. We would then put this to the EBBA as a sign (a) that we were a highly responsible club (very unlikely to be believed) and (b) there was no need for further trouble on their part (much more acceptable).

Before the EBBA disciplinary committee had chance to consider the case further, we imposed a voluntary three match ban on Larry M and a two match ban on Larry S. The former was irrelevant, since Larry was informed on the following Monday that his services were no longer required, and accepted the decision with good grace. The two match ban was lenient, but meant that Larry Sheldon would be back on court by mid-January. The plan worked. The committee even remarked on how responsible it was of us to take matters into our own hands. No one mentioned further action, no one mentioned action against the club, and no one mentioned the lack of a video. Even Mike forgot about the glass panel.

*　　*　　*

By another quirk of the fixture list, the first fixture of 1983 was the return game at Gateshead. Emergency financial measures were now in place and, following extensive analysis of the number of players entitled to a student rail card, it was decided that the team would travel by train. Being temporarily disillusioned with the team, and permanently mean with money, I didn't go with them. As a result, I can't give a first hand account of one of the most remarkable victories in the club's history.

Gateshead were unchanged from the game at Brunel, with the exception of the player suspended for his role in the altercation with Larry M, and led by their prolific American Curtis Miller, who had piled up a staggering 51 points in the first match. We, of course, were without both Larrys, and down to only nine players on the bench, which was handy as it saved a train fare.

In the absence of the two Larrys, Dave Yewman and our £100 superstar Richard Parsons were our big men. Dave scored the first three baskets, and the pair contributed 35 points between them. Most of the points, though, came from the guards. Once Phil found his range, there was no stopping him. He produced a staggering 30 points in the first half alone, as the Ducks stormed into an equally staggering 17 point lead at the interval. The second half was more even, in fact totally even at 49 points all – and the eventual winning margin 105–88.

When I heard the result, I didn't know whether to laugh or cry. It said a huge amount for both the spirit and depth of the team, and, in case anyone doubted it, showed that teams just couldn't rely on their American stars any longer. On the other hand, if a mid table team could be demolished by a nine man squad with no overseas players what could have been achieved during the rest of the season?

It was an academic question, of course, and there is no point in dwelling unduly. Nor, really, is there any point in dwelling on the rest of the season. At the time, it seemed incredibly important whether we finished in sixth, seventh or eighth place, and whether we won 11, 12 or 13 games – but there is a limit to how much detail the reader can be expected to take. The last two months were far from being a disaster; in fact we won alternate matches. But given the expectations, the season had to be regarded as a disappointment. It was hard, now, to see any way that the club could get any higher than second division security. Perhaps that should have been our aim all along.

Whatever our aspirations *should* have been, and whoever was responsible for our not achieving them, we needed to re-think our way of doing things both on and off court. One casualty of this process was Coach Tony. Almost immediately the season ended, he resigned, a victim of a tension that anyone who has ever tried to run a small team in any sport will recognise. Those of us responsible for raising the money thought it should be put to better use; the coach responsible for spending it thought that we needed more, contrasting our approach, perhaps, with that of the consortium that he had introduced to us several months earlier. Perhaps we were both right – and both wrong – at the same time.

Tony's departure was remarkable for ending a unique relationship, and starting a new one that was almost as distinctive. Whatever the tensions, he was the only coach ever to tolerate the club for more than a season. And, in a sport full of people shouting loudly, arguing passionately, bad mouthing and ridiculing each other, Tony and I pursued our differences in a very un-basketball like way. We never spoke again.

*   *   *

Until my involvement with basketball, I don't think I had seriously encountered an American. After three years, meeting our eight American players, Americans from elsewhere in the league and hundreds of English players and administrators who had mysteriously developed American accents, I felt qualified to make a full and final judgement on the country and its people.

My judgement was mixed, and in retrospect, unfair. American players were regarded, as the heroes of English basketball. Notwithstanding the Gateshead affair, they were widely seen as the guys that won games, attracted the crowds and provided the most visible distinction between national league clubs and good standard county level ones. On the other hand, they had a habit of not turning up for a full season (Dan), not turning up for games (Mike), expecting to be accommodated (everybody except Mike) and paid (everybody except Mike and Vaughan). This was a tension faced by anyone who runs a semi-professional sports team. The directors do the job for love, interest and, very occasionally, glory. For the full-time players, it is a job for which, like any other job, they need to be paid. It took me several years to appreciate the difference. In the meantime I tended to keep my distance from the American players, just in case they were about to surprise me with a rouge electricity bill.

Some people regarded my involvement with basketball as signifying a love of all things American. The Politics department at Brunel ran one of the first student exchanges with the US; through which a group of undergraduates from the State University of New York broadened their lifetime experiences with a semester in Uxbridge. Finding accommodation for a period that did not coincide with the academic year was a problem, and I was asked whether a spare room could be found in our latest rented house, in nearby Hayes End. I agreed, partly in the hope that they would be able to play basketball, partly for the novelty of seeing an American pay me (or rather my landlord) rent for a change.

Melanie and Charlene helped change my view of their race. First, they were completely different in character, whereas I had assumed that all Americans were the same. Melanie was obsessively energetic, determined to see and experience everything about the UK in as short a period of time as possible. Charlene remained deeply suspicious of anything non-American. 'There you are, copying the States again!' She once remarked while waving an *Andy Capp* cartoon from the *Daily Mirror* in my face. There really was no answer to that.

Both found our obsession with basketball, at a Lilliputian level compared with even third rate college teams in the States, to be hilarious. Never more frustratingly than when Melanie, having not played for two years, was prevailed upon to make the numbers up (illegally) for the Brunel women's team, showed up five minutes before the game, hopelessly ill-prepared and over weight, scored 20 odd points and sauntered out again, declaring that she didn't want to play regularly, having come to the UK to find out about Britain. The two of them did, however, befriend Larry S, and gave us a different perspective on Americans generally. They also proved a huge asset with our Irish landlord, a friendly and hugely credible character who was experienced in dealing with tentative English male students who feared being out on the street, but had no defence against aggressive American females, who knew that their tenure was limited to a few weeks whatever he thought.

Towards the end of their stay Melanie, fed up at my constant carping about all things American, invited us to come and stay with her family. Carol was keen, and in addition to Melanie's offer of accommodation in New York, Ian Hunt's girlfriend, Christine was undertaking an internship in Washington. I cautiously agreed, on condition, of course, that nothing could be done until after the basketball season. We eventually set off in mid March.

I was in a bad mood from the start. The basketball season had been a disappointment, I was making characteristically little progress on my doctorate and the previous day I had seen a relegation bound Rotherham lose 4–0 at Queen's Park Rangers. I was not used to six hour flights and my body clock told me that it was two o'clock in the morning when we arrived. New York was also unseasonably wet. All things considered, it was not the best time to meet Melanie's dad. An archetypal New Yorker, he was friendly, enthusiastic, effusive and absolutely convinced that his city was the best in the world.

'So, John, what do you think of the city so far?' he asked over our first dinner.

'Well, we really haven't seen anything yet. Just driven here from the airport, and stopped to look at the skyline on the way.'

'Yeah – but first impressions, what are your first impressions?'

'Well, I don't think Sunday is the best day to form any impressions', I persisted. 'Maybe I'll be better placed to answer tomorrow.'

'Sure – and you must be tired. Now John, I want you to tell me tomorrow night what you really think of this great city of ours'.

Tomorrow, when it came, was wet – very wet. Melanie was the perfect guide, but unable to make Wall Street, Greenwich Village or Time Square look anything other than ordinary, miserable and inhospitable areas undistinguishable from any other wet city in the world. To make things worse, a sudden downpour just before lunch flooded the street in which we were walking, and I tripped over a dead cat outside the subway.

'So John, you're a *real* New Yorker! So tell me, what are your impressions of our city *now*?'

'Well, the drains don't work, and no one picks up dead cats.'

There was an awkward silence. I guess I hadn't imagined just how proud New Yorkers were of their city, or how distinctive the English sense of humour can be. Either way relations with Melanie's dad were not the same for the rest of the week.

I hope that Melanie and Charlene read this book. If so, I'm sorry for being so crabby. I've now been to New York several times. It has stopped raining, and the distinctive 'buzz' about the city – which would evidently have been a good answer to the question about first impressions – is something that I now recognise. By a strange turn of fate, I have met lots of Americans in my career outside basketball, and most have been as open and friendly as you were. And none has ever asked me to pay their electricity bill.

CHEQUES AND IMBALANCES

'Y'know. I really don't think that we're going to get rid of these.'

It was the spring of 1982. Fellow director Dave and I were sorting through a ragbag of materials that constituted the club 'shop' on home match nights. Cans of drink, t-shirts, copies of *Basketball Monthly* and a lone, sad jar containing about 30 lottery tickets. The same jar, in fact, that I had been entrusted with at my first meeting some two years earlier.

Selling 470 lottery tickets had proved more difficult than expected. In the first few weeks there had been a surge in demand – occasioned by the large number of happy post-examination students on campus, the assumption that it was possible to win a worthwhile prize and the fact that I still had friends. As time progressed, such friends as I still had became wary, and it was increasingly difficult to be evasive about the fact that the top prize had gone. The jar had been relegated to increasingly remote corners of the shop, and sales had dwindled to a standstill.

No one had more emotional attachment to that jar than I did – but I had to agree. In fact, we needed to completely re-think our approach to raising funds. Hype and rumour about how we were all going to be made rich through sponsorship attracted by others had deflected the attention of clubs from getting their own house in order. Endless time was spent at committee meetings, arguing about the distribution of money which did not yet exist.

We had enjoyed some success. Around half our home games were now sponsored, in most cases without an accompanying need to hide posters or flood the campus with leaflets. No support was too small. In 1982 we announced our first drinks sponsor, Express Dairies, who duly provided us with 12 cartons of juice for the team bench at each game, three of which I routinely requisitioned to sell to the Sports Centre bar. Together with the increase in crowds, the budget was now more than double that of two years before, but expenditure was rising even faster.

Was sponsorship really the answer? Large scale sponsorship – or the presence of a non-commercial benefactor – was certainly the main difference between the big clubs at the top of Division One and those like us. But over reliance on sponsorship was leading to a 'boom and bust' situation. Big money teams tended to spend their new found wealth to the last penny, or even beyond. Once it was removed, they were as impoverished as the rest of us. Some clubs were looking to develop more stable sources of income. Hemel had been supported for some years by a lottery. West Bromwich had tried to develop a social club behind the team – a model that had kept many semi-professional football teams afloat for years. Even Solent Starts, despite their millionaire chairman, were seeking to develop new sources of income. They circulated a letter to all EBBA member clubs offering to bring their full squad to play exhibition games for an inclusive fee of £600. Since they had just whacked us by 70 odd points for free, we declined.

The normal range of student fundraising activities was quickly exhausted. On campus discos were always a winner – not because of the music or women, but because they usually came with a bar extension. In the wild, wild eighties, this could be as late as midnight. But every club and society on campus knew this, and we were restricted to about two a year. Will took our disco programme up a gear by doing a deal with the classily named Winkers Country Club, near Gerrards Cross, through which we could have the place for free on occasional Sunday or Monday nights. We were moving upmarket.

Then we discovered teddy bears. It started as a sideline. We had formed the habit of taking a mobile backboard and basket to local fetes, to let punters try their shooting skills at 10p per time. It was great promotion for the club, but each punter took too long for us to make any real money. The teddy tickets were something they could buy while waiting. It was amazing what people would do to win a bear – for their kids, girlfriends and, more often than they would admit, themselves. The only problem was that the bloody bears got everywhere. We became the only club in the league with a sack of them permanently in our office. Worse still, one or two always seemed to pop their heads out and embarrass us when we had important visitors.

You just cannot imagine the humiliation of a teddy bear falling on your head while discussing the finer points of a player contract. The bears were banished on more than one occasion, but the fact was that they had nowhere else to go.

Making them homeless would have ruined whatever image we had left. It was just the sort of issue that could have swept the campus.

*　　*　　*

In an unrelated discussion, Coach Tony had suggested that we should host an end of season club tournament. I was lukewarm about the idea, since it seemed like more work, at a time of year when we really needed to focus on fundraising, but agreed to look at what accommodation might be available at the university.

It turned out to be an idea whose time had come. Because of the sandwich system, the Brunel campus was massively underused from Easter to October, and that included much of the student accommodation. As a result of good old Margaret Thatcher, the pressure was on to develop this as a source of income but, apart from some longstanding contracts with noisy groups of Italian students who flooded the campus in July and August, professional marketing was not yet in place. During bank holiday weekends in May, many of the rooms were empty, and almost any revenue was welcomed. As a Brunel club we qualified for special rates. As a former Student Union official who had never tried to organise an illegal occupation of any part of the campus, I was considered responsible enough to take charge of the keys myself. It was a simple deal. I would take a load of keys on Friday afternoon, and return them, together with a cheque, on Tuesday morning. No staff overtime, and minimum bureaucracy. This was the 1980s at their very best.

Just about anything could have gone wrong with this arrangement, but nothing ever did. We were soon running three tournaments a year, offering the amazing deal of four nights accommodation, packed lunches and a presentation night at Winkers for the all in price of £29. Teams came from all over the place – the only conditions being that they showed up at the right time, were sociable and cleaned up their own room on pain of death. Amazingly, they all did. Tournaments proved more profitable than teddies.

Now that the idea of helping the university to promote itself by using Brunel facilities had occurred to us, we were unstoppable. Next in our sights was the Sports Centre. In the 'real' summer – by which I mean after the final year students had left in June – the campus was dead, and the sports centre no exception. I knew this because most weekends I was selected to play for the Brunel Cricket Team – so the number of able-bodied males available was certainly lower than 11.

So we invented the Hillingdon Sports Festival. The idea was simple. Chairman Mike gave us the Sports Centre free for the first weekend in July and we used every corner of it. It was modestly promoted as 'a whole new concept in community sport', and aimed not just at existing teams but offices, pubs and groups of friends. The event attracted our first ever four figure sponsor – in fact Lovell Construction sponsored the event for the rest of its history – and hundreds of participants. It was more profitable than anything we had ever done, and filled the Sports Centre to capacity on a weekend that was normally as dead as a doorpost. Mike must have been delighted – although of course you could never tell with Mike. I certainly was.

Whether the Sports Festival, or the Ducks, really helped generate business for Brunel, I don't know. Nor could I tell whether the accommodation department were really making money on our tournaments. But the flexibility of both was wonderful. This allowed us to claim that our relationship with the university was mutually beneficial, but could easily have been described as a 'hidden' form of sponsorship. I felt grateful, but not guilty. If anything, I wished that the 'sponsorship' relationship could have been even clearer.

*   *   *

Today, the idea of a university sponsoring its own basketball club would make perfect sense. Our market was exactly that which universities are trying to attract, particularly in the 16–18 age group. The community relations aspects would have been excellent, both with the local population and disadvantaged groups now prioritised by government. In an age where attracting both home and overseas students are critical to the business of the institution, the national coverage would have been valued. Today, also, Brunel is a sports university, with superb facilities including a purpose built basketball and netball facility since used by the Brunel Hurricanes, one of Britain's leading netball teams, and the sponsorship could have been linked to the university's expanding programme of sports scholarships. In 1980, none of this was in place.

The early 1980s was the worst time in the history of Brunel University to seek financial support for a basketball team. Brunel was established in 1966, a time of high expectations for higher education. The extent of these expectations could be seen from a model of the planned university which formed the centre of the Council chamber. Fourteen years later, this bore absolutely no relation to the actual. As with many of the 1960s cohort, Brunel had been given generous quantities of land, but the funds to develop it had not been forthcoming. As 1960s optimism faded into the economic crises of the 1970s, hopes of funding for major capital projects evaporated.

Within a year of the Thatcher government being elected, all kinds of previously unimaginable scenarios were being imagined. A widely circulated theory was that one or more institutions would be forced to close. In fact, the eagerly awaited grant settlement of 1981 stopped short of this last option, but still cut Brunel's annual grant by around 16 per cent – a more favourable outcome than that for some other technological universities, for whom the cuts were over twice that level.

For a trained scientist, Margaret Thatcher had very little idea about the type of culture that she was seeking to change. British academics in 1980 comprised two types of people. The first was clever and ambitious. The second was clever and lazy. Both depended on an unspoken compromise, in which salaries were lower than clever people might expect, but the work rate required was lower still. Academics hated meetings on Wednesday afternoons. They cut into two weekends.

In fact, academics had a mistrust of meetings, and management of all kinds. The main impact of the 1980s was not to cut funding, but to impose the idea that universities were organisations, rather than collections of individuals, and that such organisations needed managing. History will judge that Brunel responded more quickly than most to this challenge, providing a firm base for expansion later in the decade. This was positive in almost every respect but one. There was no spare money to sponsor a basketball team.

*   *   *

We had more success in securing support from the Student Union. Of course, to a large extent we *were* the Students Union when this story began. Or at least Debbi, having been elected vice-president for Sports, and I, as vice-president for External Affairs, were.

The Student Union, however, had its own problems. Throughout the 1970s, Student Unions had considerable independence in their spending, being simply given a fee for every student. This freedom had been exercised with enthusiasm – the Union was running at a deficit. Now, the Thatcher government was inconveniently asking not only how much money was being spent, but how much of it was being spent on political activities. Added to all this, my position with the Students Union was only for one year. The needs of the Ducks were longer term in nature.

You could see why the Thatcher government formed the impression that they were funding a hot bed of radical political activity. A quick count around the office identified posters promoting revolution in at least four continents. I never could understand why we gave up on Australia so easily. But most of the work was genuinely concerned with student welfare and educational issues. And such bizarre activities that the Student Union did support were by no means confined to politics. It was true that full-sized coaches were hired to take six people to demonstrate about all kind of causes, and even that the odd delegate had been elected to represent Brunel at conferences in Cuba. On the other hand, we also boasted the Izzy Society, whose grant was devoted to stealing mascots from other universities, and the College Appreciation Society, whose members used the union grant to visit the bars of other universities, evidently intending to compare their produce to that of Brunel. Then there was the Rag Society, whose committee spent a night in the local police cells after making a mock raid on a local bank, but forgetting to tell either the bank or the police of their plans in advance.

In these circumstances, I didn't feel too guilty about the Union supporting a basketball team. The way I saw it, the Ducks brought better sport to the campus than most expenditure under the sports budget, involved more members of the local community than most items under the external affairs budget, and provided better entertainment that most bands paid for under the entertainments budget. While I was in post, and Debbi remained sports officer, the Ducks were sure of a friendly welcome.

*   *   *

The trouble was that both Debbi and I were in post for one year only. Our successors would be appointed by that most unreliable of methods – the student union elections. These were impossible to predict. All that was needed to stand was a desire to delay entering the labour market, and two drunken signatures from the bar. There was no need for policies or experience. In fact, there was no requirement to be a real person. A year earlier my main rival had been one Wally Tharg – a student look alike from the early 1950s with old fashioned views to match. From the black and white photograph of Tharg that appeared throughout the campus, he looked as though he was in favour of corporal punishment, national service and food rationing. Tharg was remarkable for two reasons. He had contested every student union election for the past 15 years, and he did not actually exist. None of this prevented his attracting over two hundred votes.

Real life candidates divided into two categories – those who wanted to change the world and those who wanted an easy life. Neither was ideal for our purposes, but on balance the latter would be better. In reality there was little that we could do about it. Active campaigning would have been dangerous – and in any event, we didn't have a candidate to campaign for.

As things turned out, there was only one candidate for the Sports portfolio, and he didn't quite fit in either category. Graham was – well, he was a chemist. Chemists were always a bit of a rare breed at Brunel, and getting rarer by the minute. In fact, they have been extinct since the mid 1990s, when the chemistry department was closed down. In the world of student politics, they were even rarer. We had no idea what to expect.

The initial signs were good. Graham was tall, not interested in politics and talked a great game. All were advantages in basketball, but especially the talking bit. Graham was one of those enviable characters who appeared to know *something* about everything – business, money, cars, and even, we assumed chemistry, although there was relatively little evidence of this.

A typical example of Graham's persuasive skills came on the unlikely topic of goldfish. Carol and I were now sharing (different parts) of a flat near to the campus, and our common front room was shared with Carol's goldfish, Harry. To Carol, Harry had a character of his own. To me, he was old, smelly, discoloured, and, I often suspected, dead. Graham seemed the obvious person to arbitrate.

'Don't suppose you know anything about goldfish, Graham?'

'I do as a matter of fact. Used to have a part time job in a pet shop.'

'Mmm. So what do you reckon to this one of Carol's? Is he, well, *alive?*'

Graham pondered, peering in at the bowl from a variety of different angles, in the manner of a golfer lining up a championship winning put.

'Yes, he's alive. Only…'

I waited in eager anticipation. The 'only' sounded gratifyingly serious.

'…I'd say he's had a minor stroke.'

'A stroke! I've never heard anything so bloody ridiculous. Do goldfish *have* strokes?'

'Oh yes – and he could well recover. As long as he stays calm. You mustn't over excite him.'

'How the hell can he get over excited? All he does is swim around in a bowl!'

'Well, sudden changes in the environment won't help. Do you switch the light on and off regularly?'

'Graham. It's *January.* Of course we switch the light on regularly.'

'Well, that's the problem then. I'd suggest that you keep that to a minimum. In future – turn it on once a day when you come in, and off at bedtime. Keep it on in the meantime. That will help a lot.'

I knew right away that I shouldn't have asked, but the damage was done. The glimmer of hope was eagerly seized on by Carol. We were all set for a winter of high electricity bills, groping around for car keys in the dark and long periods when our sitting room was a virtual no-go area. This was all in the interests of a goldfish. The frustrating thing was that he did appear to recover – at least, as far as we could see in our dimly lit front room.

*   *   *

The same cannot be said of the Ducks finances. Safely installed in the students union, and an avid supporter of basketball (he had played at school, naturally), Graham's impact on our finances was two fold. He helped formalise student union support at £2,000 per year, and he introduced the 'magic drawer' system to manage our money.

I couldn't imagine why the magic drawer system was not implemented more widely. It was simple, cheap to administer and effective, and operated as follows. Every time you got any money, say, gate receipts or disco profits, you put it in a drawer. The drawer (in this case the top section of Graham's filing cabinet) is then locked. Every time you need money, say, to pay the players wages, you unlocked the drawer, and got it out. No paperwork, no middleman, no bureaucracy. In the decade of Margaret Thatcher, Arthur Daley and Del Trotter, it was a theory whose time had come.

Only gradually did the disadvantages dawn on us. Towards the end of the season, it was going to help to know where the money had actually gone. (The production of annual accounts was, of course, another EBBA requirement). The money was not exactly secure, and gathering dust rather than interest – and prices had risen by some 30 per cent since 1980. Perhaps most alarming of all was the realisation that the draw was not magic after all. In fact, by Christmas 2002, it was inexplicably empty. It was quickly followed by our student union grant and bank account.

The empty drawer was the symbol of our predicament, rather than the cause. Less so than other clubs, perhaps, but we had got caught up in the conventional wisdom that basketball was about to strike rich. We had gambled on the means of doing so, and the gamble had failed. Even had it not been for the two Larry's moments of madness against Gateshead, we would have had to have cut bills, and we knew it. Even limping to the end of the season would be a problem.

*   *   *

The Student Union were willing to help. They wanted us to survive, but most of all they wanted us off their hands. The deal was this. They would forget about our existing debts – but we must form ourselves into a limited company. The idea of a limited company sounded like a great wheeze. I couldn't imagine why we hadn't thought of it before.

The way I saw it, there were three big advantages of establishing Brunel Basketball Club Ltd. The first was that the EBBA already had a rule to say that all clubs must be registered as a limited company. This, of course, was regarded as the least important of the three. The second was that, when you were a limited company, there was no more arguing about who was liable for all your debts.

When you were a limited company, *no one* was liable for your debts. Wasn't that what limited liability was all about? Third, when you set up a limited company, you had capital – in our case £800 handed over by Mike (on behalf of Brunel), Will, Dave and I also became shareholders. That capital would be just enough to meet our losses in the last two months of the season. There were downsides, of course, such as the letter demanding £13 for a nice brass plaque to hang outside our office, but I wrote back to say that, since we didn't have an office, we wouldn't need that.

For reasons completely unrelated to basketball, 20 years later I become a chartered company secretary. What a revelation that was! I learned that capital had to be accounted for separately, rather than blown on the first handful of bills that arrived. I learnt too, that we *did* need to have an office – or at least something called an office. Most alarmingly of all, I learnt that company directors could be held responsible for their actions, particularly where those actions could be seen as negligent. I'm glad that I know all that now. I'm equally glad that I didn't in 1983.

So we were now a limited company. It didn't affect the huge amount of goodwill and support that we enjoyed from the Students Union – and I'd like to thank our successors, people like Simon, Hugh, Jacko, Kevin, Cecilia, Mark and Steve – and others who know who they are, but who now, in comfortable middle age, are much to ashamed to admit it, who kept supporting us in whatever way possible. And also another Steve, a former Brunel student and now chartered accountant, who took on the job not only of auditing our accounts but explaining to us what had happened in each year – or at least what we needed to say had happened if we wanted to maintain our registration.

It was a whole new world, of plaques and paperwork, shareholders and seals. It didn't make us any richer, but it made us feel somehow more permanent and business like. We were no longer a mere Committee, we were a Board. Three years late, we were ready to meet the 1980s on our own terms.

HALF-TIME ANALYSIS

The BBC once produced a documentary, comparing the 2007 FA Cup Final with that of 1957. It compared the participant's wages, game tactics, preparation and the whole way in which the players were treated. Even to the regular football fan, the intensity of preparation in 2007 was astonishing, down to the last minute of the daily schedule, or the last calorie of the personal diet.

The 1957 final was between Aston Villa and Manchester United. After six minutes, the United goalkeeper was injured – victim of an attack that today would be rated somewhere between a straight red card and a mugging. The trainer – a retired player with little or no medical background – appeared and tried to solve the problem by throwing a bucket of water over him.

When this did not work, even after vigorous sponging, the trainer declared that he had tried everything possible, and the player could not continue. Attention then moved to the next problem. This was not, as you might imagine, getting proper medical advice (the Manchester City goalkeeper had famously played on with a broken neck in the previous year's final), nor even moving the player to where such advice could be found. No, the big problem faced by the football trainer of 1957 was how to get the injured player's shirt off.

The Manchester United of 1957 only had one goalkeeper's jersey, and it was now needed. Oblivious to any long term damage that could be done, the trainer and several players hauled the hapless goalie into a upright position, tugged the reluctant shirt from his back, and presented it to the outfield player who, in an age of no substitutes, would be the replacement. The original goalie was left to walk off unaided. Happily, the story did not have a tragic ending. By the end of the first half, the goalie re-appeared – trying his luck on the wing!

*   *   *

The summer of 1983 was almost exactly halfway between the two 'extremes' of 1957 and 2007, and exactly halfway through Brunel's career as a National League basketball club. It seems reasonable, therefore, to assess how far we had moved down the road to a 'professional' approach.

The answer can be seen in the story of our first National League game of the 1983–84 season, at Gateshead. Things started well, and all the usual problems seemed to have been avoided. We had a new coach, a full squad, the bus turned up on time and it even had a video. The journey was uneventful, we had no problems finding the venue, and we strode inside full of confidence.

Unfortunately, we strode in without our kit. In the past, the coach always brought the kit in. New Coach Roy, however, despite having coached in junior basketball for the past decade, had always had someone to do this for him. No one realised this gap in his curriculum vitae until it was too late. The coach driver had driven off to rest in pastures unknown, was not expected back until after the game, and there was no such thing as a mobile phone. So it was that, on 19 September 1983, the Brunel Ducks played their first ever national league game bearing the name of a kit sponsor. The sponsor was McEwen's Lager, who also sponsored Gateshead. This was no coincidence. We were wearing their reserve strip.

*   *   *

An inability to look after the kit wasn't the only thing that was different about our new coach. Coach Roy was best known for his work with Crystal Palace juniors, who were naturally national champions. He knew virtually nothing about our club, and had never coached a men's team at senior level. He had, though, coached the women's national champions, and was the best junior coach in the country by a mile. Rightly or wrongly for someone whose life had been spent coaching women and kids, he didn't stand any back chat. He expected everyone around him to share in his dedication and commitment to the cause. Anyone who didn't simply wouldn't play – whatever the consequences.

Pre-season training in 1983 was a particularly interesting experience. Every year, we lived in the hope that a new unheralded star would simply arrive on our doorstep. We scoured the campus for any new recruit over six feet tall or with a trace of an American accent. It was a big ask that a thousand or so new male recruits, chosen for reasons completely unrelated to sport, would just happen to contain a basketball star, but blind optimism remained a central plank in our strategy

As things turned out, our strategy was right, but our timing wrong. Almost a decade later the new Brunel intake included the son of a Nigerian diplomat based in Hendon, called Michael Olowokandi. Olowokandi had not played basketball until the age of 17, but did have the advantage of being 7ft 1in tall. Within a year, he had embarked on a basketball career that took him through Pacific College in the US, to the Los Angeles Clippers, Minnesota Timberwolves and the Boston Celtics in the NBA. It is the kind of story that keeps me awake at night. In the eight years of this story, the largest transfer fee we ever received was five hundred pounds (which was still five times more than the highest we had ever paid). What could we have negotiated with the LA Clippers?

The question is academic, because there was no Michael Olowokandi among the 1983 cohort. To my surprise, through, there was one Alan Cunningham. Cunningham was not a student, but instantly recognisable, having been quite a hit in the previous season with Doncaster, then still in the First Division. He even cited the Harlem Globetrotters on his cv. From Harlem, to Doncaster, to Brunel. This guy was on a real upward trend.

And now he was a free agent, with no transfer fee payable and, better still, relatives who lived just up the road in Harrow. This, I thought, was a signal from heaven. It didn't take any knowledge of basketball to see that Al was (literally) head and shoulders above the other potential recruits, as well as being a potential crowd pleaser. Amazingly, his attitude to money seemed refreshing too. After just five minutes discussion, we concluded that we could extend our planned salary by £30 a week – on condition that he lived with his relatives and didn't charge us for accommodation. Perfect!

Coach Roy had other ideas. After intensive negotiation, I proudly announced that I had agreed potential deals with all the short listed recruits, and that he could choose any to make up his squad. I expected him to be ecstatic. Roy didn't do ecstasy.

'Well, that's good to know', he mused vaguely. 'But I'm not really sure that I want any of them'.

'Apart from Alan Cunningham, you mean?'

'I did think about him. But he might not fit in. Not sure he's a team player'.

Not a team player! Here was a guy who seemingly collected every rebound, took the ball up the court and scored most of the points himself. Did we really need a team?

Well, Roy was the coach, but it took me a long time to come to terms with this, or the alternative of returning to the previous policy of recruiting Americans 'blind'. Cunningham ended up signing for first division Worthing, doubtless at a higher salary and without the obligation of living with his mother-in-law, and he was a great success. Looking back, I guess he would have done so whatever arrangement we had come to.

So we missed out on a former Harlem Globetrotter and a future LA Clipper arrived the best part of a decade late, but Roy's stubbornness remained. Instead we recruited Jamie Weavill, a student at nearby Borough Road College, now part of Brunel. No disrespect to Jamie, who was a popular and enthusiastic member of the squad displaying all the qualities that Coach Roy sought, but it didn't seem much compensation at the time.

We were soon to find that the trend was very much against any recruitment at all. From over 30 players at pre-season training, Roy narrowed the squad down to 12, which was manageable. It then reduced itself to 10, which was tight. By November, it was down to eight, which was verging on the suicidal. No one favoured cutting costs more than I did, but this was getting ridiculous.

*   *   *

By the time we got to Gateshead, we had not only mislaid the kit, but one of the two Americans recruited to wear it. Conscious of our past problems in this department, in 1983 we had decided to do things properly. We recruited two players, Nick and Brian, from the same US college, assuming that this would reduce the chances of homesickness. We also decided to offer VIP treatment from the outset.

VIP treatment really wasn't our thing. On the one hand, it was good that Carol and I went personally to meet them at the airport. On the other, Carol's car was a mini, and Brian was 6ft 10in tall. Then, on arrival back at our flat, both Brian and Nick got their first introduction to cricket. For Yorkshire to win their first trophy in 15 years, I explained breathlessly, they either had to beat Essex, or it had to rain all day. The latter, of course, was much more likely. Both looked on in bemusement at my increasing delight at what was probably the most miserable weather that they had ever seen. I guess we didn't create the right impression after all. Within two weeks Brian had slipped a disc and was returning to the airport. This time, he travelled by taxi.

Brain's replacement, Micah, was a mere six feet nine. We had signed him blind on a recommendation from Tulane University, and in our haste to get him to Gateshead, had booked his air ticket from New Orleans, two days before our first game, simply on the knowledge that he lived somewhere in Louisiana. For once, we had been lucky. Louisiana is a big place, but Micah happened to live within 10 miles of the airport. He made the plane, the bus to Gateshead and started the game off with a spectacular dunk. Then reality set in. Playing with an unfamiliar kit might have been overcome; playing with an unfamiliar team could not. For the fifth season out of five we started with a defeat.

Worse was to follow. Although the team got its first league points of the season with a 10 point win over Bradford the following week, the early stages of the season were the most frustrating period of this entire story. We had not started the season with the expectations of the previous year, and we were not spending the same budget. But we did have a decent team, and expected to hold our own. And so we always did. Until, it seemed, the last crucial minutes of each game.

Next up, after the Bradford game, was Colchester. We led at half-time, went to sleep early in the second half and, although we were never more than nine points behind, frustratingly lost by four. At Newcastle, another half-time lead turned into defeat. The following week, Camden were the visitors. Again we led at half-time. This time we extended our lead in the second half, but still Camden came back, taking the lead for the first time by sinking two free throws with literally no seconds left on the clock. By the time we went to Watford, in the second week of November, we positively dreaded being ahead at half-time. Sure enough, a three point interval lead was converted into a two point defeat, this time with the added ingredient of Coach Roy being reported to the league for complaining that the clock was going too fast. I couldn't help thinking that, far from being too short, second halves were generally too long. In fact, I was starting to believe that they were an absolute menace.

By mid-November, we were in danger of being the only team in the history of basketball to finish bottom of the league, but still have a positive points difference. This really wasn't very much consolation. Our record showed one win and six defeats and most people didn't look beyond these two columns. Certainly not the EBBA, who instead of focussing on my proposal to reduce the length of games from 40 to 20 minutes (back dated to the start of the season) chose precisely this time to announce that they were considering the establishment of a third division. It didn't need a genius to work out that we were prime candidates.

*   *   *

It wasn't only wins that were becoming scarce. The players were disappearing, too. Some said that Coach Roy treated them like kids. Coach Roy said that some behaved like kids. Either way, by the start of November we were struggling to field a full bench of 10 players. Worse still, the players that had left were disproportionately big ones.

In many walks of life (such as fishing), size not only matters, but varies according to who you are talking to. Basketball is no exception. This even applied to 'smaller' players. Looking through match programmes, I see Phil variously described as anything from 5ft 9in to 6ft 2in, depending on whom we were trying to impress, and how well we knew them. But while Phil's height was somewhat adjustable, there was no hiding the lack of height elsewhere. Following the sudden disappearance of Dave Yewman, we were missing this badly. Apart from Nick and Micah, we relied on Ian, now a veteran in his fourth season, and Andy Robbie, a student who had never played at National League level before.

Worse still, we couldn't always rely on Ian, who now combined his playing role with that of coach of our new National League ladies team. The two roles were normally compatible, since home games were played as double headers. Also, whereas the majority of men's national league teams played on Saturday nights, most women's sides favoured Sunday afternoons. Nonetheless, it wasn't a role that appealed to Coach Roy's puritanical tendencies. He would often show his disapproval by not using Ian in the early stages of games where he had been coaching immediately beforehand.

The tension came to a head in early December, in determining the team to play our first ever weekend double header on the road – at Merseyside and Bradford. Having at last managed a close win in the home game against Merseyside the previous weekend, it was vital that we maintain momentum – but this thought didn't seem to have stuck either Coach Roy or Ladies Coach Ian. With the Ladies team due to host league leaders Bath at the same time that we were due on court in Merseyside, Ian maintained that, although he was willing to travel with the men's team, he could only do so if the club decided that this was the best course of action. Coach Roy's view, as ever, was that he didn't *ask* players to play for him under any circumstances. It was for Ian to decide what he wanted to do. Meanwhile we were down to seven players.

Something had to be done. The best I could get out of Roy was that he would be willing to play Ian, but only if I raised the issue. The best I could get from Ian was that he would be willing to come, but only if I told the women. Thus, despite the presence of two basketball coaches with a combined height of 13ft, it fell to me to break the unpopular news. The recipients were not happy, considering it another example of how their interests were trampled on by those of the men, and pointing out that, having won three games, they had already made more progress in their first National League season than the men had four years previously.

The decision to take Ian turned out to be the right one, for three reasons. First, the game against Bath was lost by 73–33; Ian could have played, let alone coached, and still not made any difference to the result. Second, because Everton Park, new home of the Merseyside club, and located in one of the less predictable parts of the city, was not a place to be without big men – either on or off court. Third, and most important, it was justified because the weekend proved to be a turning point for the entire season.

We led Merseyside by seven points at half-time. Not that this was of much comfort, given our experience of the season to date. Sure enough, the first five minutes of the second half were a disaster. After Nick has extended the lead to 10, with a basket and free throw, we conceded 19 points to six. In the middle of the crisis, Micah conceded his fourth and fifth fouls in quick succession. We were going to have to win the game with seven players after all.

And so we did. There were never more than three points in it until the last two minutes, when two baskets from Phil, two from Mike and one from Ian pulled us away to a flattering eight point margin of victory. It was a genuine team effort – seven of our eight players scored five points or more. Ian was responsible for 12. The momentum carried over to the following day, which produced a single point win at Bradford. No matter that this time Nick and Micah, making up for his early exit of the previous day, contributed almost two-thirds of the points, no matter that the match officials needed an escort from the court following their decisions late in the game; no matter, even, that I got so carried away in my celebrations that I left the all important player registration cards in the bar after the game. This had been a good weekend.

The atmosphere on the team coach back to London was as good as I can ever remember. Even Ian seemed pleased that he had made the journey. 'Now we know how to win', he explained to Carol and I somewhere between Nottingham and Leicester 'there'll be no stopping us'.

None of us could know just how right this would turn out to be.

*   *   *

In the wider world, the state of delusion and gullibility reached new heights in 1983. In March, President Reagan had told us that his new 'star wars' initiative would keep us safe from nuclear attack, as long as we stayed friends with America, of course. In April, we were fooled by the publication, in the *Sunday Times,* no less, of what turned out to be a fake set of diaries from Adolf Hitler. In June, we elected another Conservative government.

The Conservative manifesto looked good for the Ducks. Small businesses, it declared, were the route to economic recovery. It was vital to create the conditions in which new companies could thrive and expand. The right environment was essential. Conservatives would remove the barriers to growth, such as excessive regulation and red tape.

Electoral experts noted that this message was much more popular in the south of the England than the north. They were right. It certainly didn't penetrate as far as Leeds or, more precisely, the headquarters of the English Basket Ball Association. Oblivious to the new climate of deregulation, the EBBA re-doubled its efforts to impose minimum standards – of capacity, lighting, space, changing rooms – you name it. Needless to say, we met hardly any of them, although we still had a good scoreboard.

This particular small business was keen to expand – but not if said expansion involved a move away from Brunel University. The problems of 1982–83 had increased our belief in a cautious approach, in which we paid for as little as possible, and devoted as much as possible of what we did pay towards playing costs. A quick tour around Harrow Leisure Centre – a splendid venue which wanted to charge virtually our entire gate revenue in court fees – confirmed that this was only really possible at Brunel.

A move outside the London Borough of Hillingdon, we argued, was not feasible in the short term, as it would involve generating a whole new fan base at the same time as incurring substantial extra cost. Moreover, it would mean that 'Brunel' were no longer, well, Brunel. This met with grudging acceptance, but a requirement that we still explore reasonable alternatives within the borough.

I figured that this would be easy to meet, because the words 'reasonable' and 'the London Borough of Hillingdon' were widely regarded as being incompatible. Hillingdon politics were quite different to those of Doncaster. In the Doncaster of the 1970s, everybody knew their place. Labour were in power, the Conservatives in opposition and the Liberals were delivering leaflets complaining about them both. This truth was maintained election, after election, after election. Cosy relationships developed which later made 'Donnygate' a by-word for local government corruption, but these did have the virtue of getting the business out of the way quickly. As part of my doctoral study, the taxpayer had funded at least one three hundred mile round trip to observe a meeting of the Doncaster Education Committee. A round trip from Uxbridge of over six hours, to observe a meeting that was completed within seven minutes, with not a single question being asked.

In Hillingdon, things were different. Not only did both parties have expectations of running the Council, but, unlike Doncaster, the whole Council was elected in a single go every four years. Huge swings in policy were the norm, aided by a host of strong personalities. For the much of the 1970s, Hillingdon was portrayed in the national media as the archetypal wasteful Labour authority, spending money on every cause imaginable, and many that were not. By the mid-1980s it had a Conservative administration that earned equal notoriety for not spending money, typified by a well publicised decision to bus immigrants out of the borough, rather than house them.

The Conservative administration may have created problems for immigrants and schools, but it was ideally suited to our current predicament. Of course, it was irritating that there was no prospect of the large grants available to basketball teams in the inner London boroughs. On the other hand there was absolutely no prospect that it was going to do anything as rash as build a leisure centre that could be used to force us away from Brunel. Inactivity, I felt sure, was one characteristic that I could rely on.

*   *   *

Anxious to give the impression that no stone was being left unturned, I presented myself at a meeting of the London Borough of Hillingdon Sports Advisory Committee. The Committee was an advisory body to a sub-committee of the Leisure Committee, which itself was a sub-committee of the Council – in turn a body with little money and no inclination to spend it. Its rationale reminded me of an explanation given by a particularly well travelled academic for his tendency to attend so many international conferences. 'Individually', he explained, 'we can do nothing'. 'Together, we can agree that nothing can be done'.

My strategy was to state our problem in a sincere but lukewarm fashion to the Committee, and then reluctantly accept, in the best traditions of local government, that 'nothing could be done' and retire to the pub with a contrived sigh of resignation. Within minutes, I found to my horror that I had been co-opted as the basketball representative for the borough. There was nothing for it. I would have to sit through the entire meeting, and probably more besides.

Worse still, the committee started to display a frustrating interest in the problem. Plans were being drawn up, apparently, for a major leisure development (privately financed, naturally) at a site just off the A40 and about three miles away from Brunel. Happily, these were some years from fruition (in which state they were to remain for a further two decades). In the meantime, some kind of interim arrangement was needed. The new look Hillingdon Council was proud of its ability to whiz around finding low cost answers for problems that had baffled bureaucrats for years.

After half an hour of highly sophisticated discussion, I was asked to explain the differences between basketball and netball. As I was doing so, an elderly member leaned back in his chair and announced with a huge sigh of satisfaction announced that he had a solution. It was, he explained, a simple matter of thinking outside the box. Or, in this case, outside the entire building. His suggestion was that we should play our games outside. Like the netball girls did.

To my horror, the idea was greeted with enthusiasm. There were, after all, plenty of outdoor facilities in the borough. Some even had floodlights. These would offer much more flexibility for erecting temporary seating and accommodating television requirements. I even stared to fantasise myself. The position of match promoter would henceforth become much more important. The pre-match toss-up would no longer just decide which team would play towards the clock in the second half. It would involve complex calculations about wind direction, ground conditions and the possibility of rain. Most of all, I fantasised about the reaction of the English Basket Ball Association, when I told them that, at their request, I had explored all options for moving the team elsewhere in Hillingdon, and that this was the plan that we had come up with.

Back in the real world, I confined myself to a polite response. Rather than giving a detailed description of the game, or trying to justify why seven feet tall basketball players were more pampered than five foot netball girls, I simply resorted to saying that such an arrangement was outside the rules. But that I was very grateful for their interest, and looked forward to a long and close relationship with the committee.

In fact, I was wrong. I checked the rules the following day. Despite going into minute detail on the size of court, seating arrangements, access to changing facilities, conduct of the pre-match toss up and standard of sandwiches, the rules actually said nothing about the need for a roof. It was a missed opportunity of heroic proportions.

*   *   *

The start of 1984 was an exciting time, both for the club and for us personally. Carol had a new job undermining the government's economic strategy by bringing in lots of cheap imports from the Far East. In January, she went on her first ever business trip to Hong Kong, paranoid about eating 'real' Chinese food. She duly got food poisoning – on the British Airways fight home. In

February, we won the top prize in the Ducks 100 club lottery, which I was naturally going to donate back to the club, but Carol got there first, muttering something about a washing machine.

I had to give way on the washing machine issue, because in the same month we bought our very first flat. The existence of a large sitting room all to ourselves signalled the start of a new late night Saturday night ritual, which would see the two of us spread out on the floor counting the gate money. Some people might regard this as an aphrodisiac – I imagine that thought will cross the mind of our Hollywood producer. We didn't see it that way. In fact, on more than one occasion it led to a blazing row when we were 30 quid short of the amount that we thought the crowd had merited.

On court, the team had really learned how to win. They followed up the northern tour with successive victories over Colchester, Plymouth, Newcastle and Nottingham. But as we had found in our only previous good run a couple of years ago, winning was very much an acquired art, for supporters as well as players. For three months, virtually every game had been on a knife edge until the last minute, so we forgot how to relax. At the very same moment as Carol was getting food poisoning on her flight home from Hong Kong, Mike Short's wife Paula and I were having a nervous breakdown every time Plymouth hit the basket in our first away game of 1984. It didn't matter that we were 28 points in the lead with just two minutes to go – experience told us that something was about to go wrong.

*   *   *

It is a central theory of this book that the fortunes of basketball are intertwined with developments in the wider world. Nowhere was this more the case than the transformation of the Brunel Ducks fortunes in late 2003 and early 2004. I can now reveal my previously unpublished thesis that the credit for this should go to none other than US President Ronald Reagan. Reagan, it will be remembered, owed us a favour following the sudden disappearances of his employee Mike McLarin three years previously. In my view, his well publicised 'star wars' policy of 1983 went some way to discharging this debt.

The implications of 'star wars' to basketball were obvious. The policy was based on the theory that getting involved in a 'shoot out' – even if you had the strongest weapons – could lead to unforeseen, maybe disastrous consequences. That had been exactly our problem in the earlier part of the season. A safer policy was to stop the opposition shooting at you at all, so that whatever fire power you had could be used at leisure. Applied to international relations, this involved the creation of a huge shield around the United States that missiles could not penetrate. Applied to basketball, it meant doing the same thing around your own basket.

The extent to which Coach Roy was influenced by this debate can be seen in our two matches against Sandwell, the eventual league winners. In the away game, in November, we had scored 116 points – our highest score of the season. Unfortunately, Sandwell piled up an outrageous 132. It was a shoot-out that we were destined to lose from the outset, mainly because Sandwell had an outstanding American guard who never missed. It seemed to me that he had scored about 120 points on his own.

By the time of the return, in late January, the Coach Roy/President Reagan theory was fully operational. It decreed that Sandwell were not going to get 132 points at Brunel, because they were not going to get the ball often enough. Brunel were dictating the pace of the game, and Sandwell were getting frustrated. We led by 39–36 at half-time. The pressure increased further when said American guard fouled out with six minutes to go and the scores level at 63 all, followed by a technical foul on the Sandwell bench. We were convinced that we were on the verge of victory. Since Sandwell were destined for the first division, and had just won 17 games on the bounce, it would have been our biggest scalp to date.

In fact, it wasn't, but the 69–73 final score demonstrated the extent to which we had improved, and history will (or at least should) record that the star wars theory ultimately had more impact on basketball than it did on promoting world peace. The Sandwell game proved to be one of only two defeats in the second half of the season. The other, by a single point in the home game against Gateshead, would have been avoided had a last second shot from Jamie not rolled agonisingly around the rim before bouncing out.

After losing seven games out of the first nine, we recovered to win 13 out of the last 15, taking fifth place out of 13 teams in the league. It was a remarkable turn around by any standards. Certainly it was too much for the EBBA, who coincidentally abandoned their plan to create a third division as soon as it was clear that we were not going to be in it.

Moreover, the transformation was achieved without any influx of players. The happy breed of eight that embarked on the northern tour in December remained the core team. They were joined in the second half of the season by Pete Fish, a player from the Brunel local league squad, and there were even occasional appearances by Tony, making a transition from coach to player that I could not imagine of any current premier league football manager. Perhaps Coach Roy's theories about only dealing with players who genuinely wanted to play were not so bad after all. On the other hand, I would not want to underestimate the historical role of a shy, naturally modest guy like Ronald Reagan.

An improvement to fifth place in the league was not hugely significant in itself, but the legacy of 1983–84 shouldn't be under estimated. A year before we had been on a downward trend, disappointed that our assault on promotion had been rebuffed so easily, and cautious about trying anything so rash again. By March 1984, the smiles and optimism had returned. Even the most optimistic of us could not have imagined how far these would be justified.

*　　*　　*

Even after the last ball had been thrown in anger, the season had one further twist. I approached the end of season league meeting smug in the knowledge that we had once again defied the forces of money and logic. We had survived another season with league place, bank balances and even our dissident kit in tact. I should have known not to be so sanguine.

The league authorities had long considered that each club should have a physical office, presumably to ensure that the increasing volume of bills, legal actions and league circulars announcing new regulations were properly directed. This in itself had not seemed to be a problem. We duly installed a desk in the Sports Centre, within hearing distance of a telephone, and sent the details to Leeds.

Now, judging from a hidden corner of the meeting papers, this remorseless pursuit of professionalism had reached new heights. Henceforth, the office would have to be occupied by a person, and, preferably, a person with some knowledge of the club. We tried to compromise in our most conciliatory manner. We even offered to invest in new technology, but were rebuffed. An answer phone simply wouldn't do.

My long suffering doctoral supervisor might argue differently, but I was not a full-time basketball employee, and not in a position to become one. Nor could the sports centre staff be trusted to answer random phone messages pretending to be club officials. Some of them had an unhealthy tendency towards honesty. Of course, the idea of a paid administrator was unthinkable, and the idea of an unpaid employee seemed to have been ruled out by the decision of a previous Tory administration, almost two hundred years previously, to abolish slavery. Or perhaps not…

The Thatcher government, it seemed, was serious in its promise to help small business. A letter arrived in the Sports Centre, announcing a new version of the Youth Training Scheme. This was designed to provide subsidised employment opportunities for young people and, no doubt as an afterthought, reduce the rapidly expanding unemployment figures. The letter was not signed by Margaret Thatcher personally, but by a local employment agency, in conjunction with Uxbridge College. Nor was it addressed to me personally, but to Mike, in his capacity as Director of the Sports Centre. Having intercepted it from his desk, however, I took it as a personal invitation from the Prime Minister to play my part in easing the national problem of unemployment, while at the same time pursuing her favourite philosophy of self-help.

The deal on offer reflected all that was best in Thatcherism. A new form of employment involving low pay, long hours, no security of employment, regular support for the employer and no prating around with trivia such as tax and national insurance contributions. More precisely, an eager young employee for £10 a week, typically for a year but with capacity to terminate at just about any time. Minor irritants included the need to give day release for training, the option to pay travel costs in addition and the need to attend occasional sessions with a supervisor. I was assured that these were as much for the benefit of the employer than the trainee.

I had some moral qualms. Finding work for a trainee would be no problem, offering effective supervision, when the club had no other employees, might be. The training element might be a problem for us both. An unenthusiastic student might not find enough material to write a proper project, an intelligent one might find too much, and embarrass us. There was also the question of whether we could trust someone with no experience, no proven aptitude for the work and who would be gone within a year.

Keen to close the deal, the College sent details of an ideal possibility. The club liked Sally because she was a keen netball player, and already knew some of the Brunel women's team. Mike liked her because she was a sports fanatic, who could no doubt be called upon to do other things. I liked her because she didn't complain about much and was cheap. In fact, she lived and had been to school within a mile of the Brunel campus, so that even the optional travel costs could be managed, or even eliminated if I could persuade her of the benefits of jogging to work. We agreed to go ahead.

I saw Sally last year. She gave me a card which announced her as Head of Facilities at the massively expanded Brunel Sports Centre, where she had just completed 25 years continuous service.

WINDS OF CHANGE

1984 promised to be a year of change – for the country, for me and for the Brunel Ducks in particular.

The Thatcher government amended its philosophy. For five years, they had told us that everyone could be rich, as long as they worked hard. Now, since this had not made them universally popular, they removed the bit about work. Henceforth, everyone could be rich – full stop. If you were lazy, you could sit back and watch the value of your property rise. For the more energetic, filling a few forms and writing a cheque bought you a succession of shares that were virtually guaranteed to rise in value. Floatation of the newly privatised British Telecom, in November 1984, was to be a sign of things to come.

Carol and I embraced this philosophy with enthusiasm. Not only did we both buy our quota of British Telecom shares, but we were settled in our new flat, thanks to a joint mortgage from the Woolwich Building Society, who were seemingly oblivious to the fact that I had no guaranteed source of income beyond the next nine months. Not that we threw caution to the wind completely. The flat had one and a half bedrooms – just in case things didn't work out.

The lack of any guaranteed income after September may not have worried the Woolwich Building Society, but it did worry me. After three years of study, my doctorate was nowhere near completion, while the academic job market was perilous even for the few PhD candidates that did complete. The world outside academia, with its quaint expectations of employees that turned up at regular intervals, was too horrible to contemplate.

Fortunately, my supervisor had been using his time more effectively than I had. He had just been awarded yet another research project. This one, ironically, would investigate how higher education could become more relevant to the labour market. He could not recall my producing any work of sub-standard quality over the previous three years – or indeed any other quality – and asked whether I would be interested. The job sounded ideal, with three years security, academic hours and pay scales, and a location within a few hundred yards of the Sports Centre. Even the well meaning but somewhat menacing threat of time off to complete my doctorate could not deter me.

*   *   *

Not anticipating this development, I had told the club that I may have to retire. Not definitely, but enough to generate the presentation of a pewter mug with an inscription thanking me for all my hard work. Even had it not been for the job situation, retirement from basketball management at the grand old age of four seasons had its attractions. I was at the age where most people believe that any experience is a good experience. Perhaps the 'achievement' of helping a basketball team stay afloat for what was already longer than the average period should simply be banked, and I should move on to something else.

The problem was – *what* else? If ever there was a time to re-kindle my interest in politics, this was it. March 1984 had seen the start of a national coal strike, regarded both by the National Union of Mineworkers and the government as a critical test of the Thatcher administration. I didn't have to depend on the national media for updates. My dad worked at a colliery, he took early retirement shortly afterwards as part of the deliberate run down of the industry; my home village was on the border between the pro-strike South Yorkshire and anti-strike Nottinghamshire coalfields; the colliery in the village where I had gone to school was on the verge of closure. I knew from the accounts of my parents – just about the least political family in the region – how bitter and personal events were becoming – not only against the government, but working miners and, increasingly, the behaviour of the police.

I'm ashamed to say that, even with one degree in politics and another on the way, I couldn't think of any practical way of responding to this situation, beyond moaning and contributing to collections. I would have been even less use on a picket line than a basketball court. Nor did I have any confidence that political activity would make much difference. The Labour Party themselves only offered lukewarm support. In any event, there was no prospect of them being elected. We were still a year from Neil Kinnock's speech to the 1985 Labour Party Conference, widely seen as the first turning point in their fortunes. In the meantime the Labour Party, and I, sat impotent as an industry that had helped to mould both of us was destroyed.

My return to basketball became inevitable. For the first game of the season,

December 1981 – Bob Spencer finds his way to the basket in the home game against Bolton – but Ducks still went thirteen points behind in the first half.

December 1981 – a happier looking crowd in the second half as American Bob Barry finds the basket...

...and Dave Anderson rises above the Bolton defence. Ducks recovered to win by six.

Bob Barry contests the ball with Bolton's Spychalla (12) and Eadsforth (13).

March 1982 – The team that learned how to win. Brunel line up for their final league game against Nottingham. Back row: Bob Senior, Richard Parsons, Bob Spencer, Dave Anderson, Bob Berry, Coach Tony Harrison. Front row: Nigel Walters, Ian Cohen, Ian Hunt, Phil Ralfe.

February 1984 – Jamie Weavill (top) and Micah Blunt (bottom) get shots away during the league win over Plymouth Raiders. Raiders were so impressed that they signed Micah for the following season.

Brian Kellybrew – one of the few Americans to tolerate life with the team for a second year – to the delight of Directors and female fans alike.

Autumn 1984 - Time out for Perry and Eric - the most under stated, under rated and under paid overseas players in the League.

Autumn 1983 – A study in determination. Brunel women's team enter the National League for the first time. They took just two months to better the men's win tally in their first season, and secured the club's first shirt sponsorship deal with freight company Arkle. Brunel players pictured are Fiona Foster (passing) and Phil Clancy.

November 1980. Defence – what defence? Brunel hardly know which way to look as Solent Stars guard Jim Guymon sets up yet another basket. The Ducks 50-121 defeat was the heaviest in league history.

October 1980. Wham! Two more points for Mike McLarin in a National Cup win over Camden – my first ever home match as Club Promoter. Bob Hill looks on.

January 1985 – The crunch game against Calderdale – and the pressure is telling. Brunel's Eric Clarke (under the basket) is poised for a rebound. Perry Smith (15) and Dave Yewman (12) look on.

Summer 1986 – Clearly the right decision! Brian Kellybrew and a menacing look-ing Dale Roberts accept the Ducks award as Hillingdon's Sports team of the Year, from the Director of double glazing company Allglass.

March 1985 – 'Next Home Match – Division One! The Brunel team that won promotion. Back row players include Dave Yewman (12), Andy McGivern (14), Eric Clarke (13), Perry Smith (15). Front row: Mike Short (6), Anton Ferris (10), Tony Marcovski (9), Phil Ralfe (5), Steve Ball (8) and Neil Clark (7). Coach Mark Dunning is second from right on the back row.

November 1982 – Dave Yewman (35), Larry Sheldon (34) and Ian Cohen (24) and all five Newcastle players search in vain for a rebound. The long range shot from Phil Ralfe (partially obscured at the rear) found the basket. Phil scored 20 points, and the Ducks won by 94-80.

Nightmare against Solent (continued). Yet another loose ball seems destined for a white shirt – despite the best efforts of Jeff Johnson (32), Frank Bartram (41, obscured), Graham Silman (33) and Bob Hill (31).

Eric won more than his share of rebounds in the promotion winning season of 1984-85 – but it's hard to see how he is going to win this one.

I simply turned up as a spectator. For the second, I took my PhD notes to the library on the Saturday afternoon, and said that I might drift across for the game later. The game tipped-off at 8pm, and I was there by 4pm. For the third game, I simply reported for duty as normal.

*   *   *

Changes were coming thick and fast for the Ducks, too. Most alarmingly, the kit had disappeared. It was officially stolen, but I was suspicious. What market could there possibly be for a five-year-old kit? Moreover, this was the only kit in England with Ducks written on the back and the numbers 21-42. It would be harder to sell than a Van Gough. It looked to me like a robbery to order. Either an inside job from fashion conscious players, or inspired by EBBA officials, incensed that their generosity at Macclesfield four years earlier was being abused.

'You think more of that bloody kit than you do of the players', shouted our recently appointed team manager, Ossie. He was right, of course. The kit had cost nothing (at least during my tenure), turned up for every game (apart from the Gateshead fiasco) and never made the slightest complaint. Protest, though, was useless. The kit was gone and there was bound to be a league rule against playing naked. This was a very bad start.

We also had a new coach. Coach Roy's popularity during his year in charge had not been confined to his eight players, but extended to the club as a whole, particularly as results had improved. His heart, though, was still in junior basketball, and also at Crystal Palace, rather than tedious trips round the M25 and his day job as an IT lecturer. When the prospect was held out of a salary to act as administrator for the club, he decided that the opportunity was too good to miss. In fact, it was also too good to believe. Crystal Palace were about to embark on yet another financial crisis.

We did not have to look far for a replacement. Although still in his late twenties or early thirties, Coach Mark seemed to have been around in basketball for ever. He had been involved with the Greenford Cardinals, one of Brunel's traditional rivals at Middlesex League level, for as long as I could remember, and increasingly become involved at regional and national level. He was wildly enthusiastic, and more extrovert than Coach Roy, but both had one thing in common – basketball was their life.

Nowhere was this more vividly demonstrated than in Coach Mark's training night routine. Training at Brunel was from 8.30pm to 10.30pm on Tuesday and Thursday. Coach Mark would be there at least an hour in advance, for meetings with such players or club officials as would talk to him. To the chagrin of sports centre staff who wanted to lock the building, he would stay for more individual meetings afterwards. He would then travel home, and call a range of friends and contacts in the States for advice on how the night had gone. Then, as an afterthought, he would call me. By this time, it could be one or two o'clock in the morning.

'Hello?'

'Hey John. It's Mark!'

'Um.'

'Thought I'd let you know how training went tonight'

'Um.'

'You'll never guess who showed up?'

'Mark – at this time of night it had better be the Queen. And only then if she was carrying a big cheque.'

'Nearly right. It was Dave Yewman.'

'Ahh.'

'Thought you'd like to know. Well, best get to bed now. Night.'

'Night, Mark.'

This was one of our better conversations, and Mark was right. The re-emergence of Dave Yewman, who had played an important role two years previously but dropped out during the early days of Coach Roy's tenure, was preferable to a visit from the Queen, all the more so since the Queen famously never carries money. Dave was joined by Neil Clark, another of Roy's junior protégés at Crystal Palace, and Andy McGivern, a 6ft 4in or 6ft 6in forward (depending on whose programme you read) student who had played for British Colleges. On the other hand, Jamie Weavill was no longer studying locally, and had been lured to Halifax, and Ian Hunt had decided to undertake a teaching qualification in the South West. Coach Mark also recruited some of the better local league players such as Chris Chappell and Tony Markowski. Gone were the days of eight man benches. There were two new Americans, too. Eric and Perry were our first paid all-black combination, but their temperament couldn't be more different. Eric was the more outgoing and outwardly friendly. Perry was quiet, thoughtful but potentially, as we were to find out, devastating in some quite unpredictable ways.

*   *   *

Even the rules were changing, with the introduction of the 'three point basket', for long distance shots. In typical Brunel fashion, we tried to avoid rule changes for as long as possible, so it was our third game before we actually scored one. We also started the season with our first 'home' game away from Brunel – an out of term National Cup tie at the Montem Centre in Slough. This was part of our strategy to persuade EBBA that we were taking the possibility of a change in home court seriously, without actually doing much about it. As if to warn us against taking the policy too far, we lost. We did, however, win our first league game, against a new team from Swindon. For the first time in National League history, the Ducks league record read 'Played One, Won One'.

Next up were Tyneside, one of two 'merged' teams in the league, having brought together the Newcastle and Gateshead sides of the previous season. The other was Calderdale, which had absorbed Bradford. Since all four sides had been strong in their own right, their successors were clear favourites for the two promotion slots that the EBBA had at last agreed would (probably) be available, provided that no one disliked the two candidates (too much). I would like to think that this new policy was a triumph for my negotiation skills as the Division Two representative on the National League Committee. More likely, it was down to money. Since the great plans for joint marketing deals had collapsed, together with weekly television coverage, there was little left for the so called elite to protect.

For most of the game, there seemed little prospect of an upset. We were 10 points down by halfway through the second half. Then Tyneside ran out of steam. The crowd sensed it was happening, and roared not only every Brunel basket, but every steal and rebound. Tyneside scored only five baskets in the last 10 minutes, and none in the last three. Coach Mark's emphasis on defence was even stronger than Coach Roy's – but the key element was depth. Tyneside used just six players in the whole game, Brunel all 10. When Mike Short scored to level things up in the last minute, five of the six last Brunel baskets had been scored by different players – not including Perry. Once in extra-time, there was no looking back. We were never behind again, and ran out winners by three points.

*   *   *

Not content with closing down the coalfields, the Thatcher government were experiencing problems closer to home – which they naturally regarded as the South East. With most of the Metropolitan Police reportedly taunting striking miners in Yorkshire, there was a danger that crime would run rampant. Protecting the aspiring middle class – respectable, property owning Company Directors such as, well, me – was vital to the whole Thatcher project.

We experienced this phenomenon in October, with our first ever league visit to Tower Hamlets. Tower Hamlets was, by common acclaim, just the sort of place where basketball should expand, an inner city area rich in talent, potential and Council grants. It was a Sunday afternoon game, so we took the opportunity of going by car, and stopping off to see some of the famous East End markets on the way.

We intended to make some shrewd purchases for the flat. Instead, we became transfixed with a guy selling chocolates. He had boxes and boxes of them – all brand names, as far as we could see – and he was piling them up into a big sack. As soon as someone bid a fiver, the sack was theirs. The boxes were being thrown in thick and fast, and on impulse we decided to buy a sack to supplement our Christmas presents. We were, of course, oblivious to sell by dates. In the Britain of the 1980s, such petty regulation was for wimps.

By half past five, I concluded that it had been a good day. We had negotiated a great deal on chocolates, Tower Hamlets looked like relegation candidates and the game produced a comfortable win. I was wrong on two counts. Tower Hamlets were destined to play a critical role in the future direction of the season. Second, on returning to the car we found that there were no chocolates left to enjoy. They had disappeared, together with the passenger seat windows.

The local policeman to whom we reported this outrage decreed that it was almost certainly the act of kids. He wearily assured us that an urgent search would be launched for a group of nine-year-olds with stomach ache, and that he would let us know if there were any developments. Immediate progress sounded unlikely, so we returned somewhat crestfallen to Harrow on a windy

Autumn evening at an average speed of 20 miles an hour, with two windows missing.

I proudly reported this story to anyone who would listen. It was my own personal experience of the horrors of Thatcherism – a tale of how the once proud, honest working class of East London had been driven by despair to a life of crime. I may even have embellished it a little. Our thieves may have become visible, they might have doubled in age, even acquired some offensive weapons – that sort of thing. I even fed the news into the political system, at the next meeting of the London Borough of Hillingdon Sports Advisory Committee. I felt very strongly about our chocolates.

To my surprise, the political system responded quickly. I would have been happy with some form of compensation, perhaps a small public enquiry. The Thatcher government, though, was in no mood for half measures. By 15 December the House of Commons had passed an entirely new Act, completely reforming local the Government in London, and abolishing the entire Greater London Council.

This seemed to me like a bit of an over reaction. Frankly, the chocolates weren't worth that much. Moreover, the new legislation not only affected London – it abolished six other county councils – all, strangely, Labour controlled. How on earth could, for example, the West Yorkshire County Council be blamed for my problems? Perhaps it was the politician still lurking inside me, but I was inclined to look for other motives.

*   *   *

My suspicions proved correct. It became clear that the Thatcher government had deeper reasons for eliminating a troublesome layer of local government. As the miners were finding, Margaret Thatcher knew how to bear a grudge, and since the election of a Labour GLC three years earlier, it had given her plenty of opportunity to develop one. London developed its own policy on everything from badgers to bus fares, and that policy was invariably at odds with that of the Government. Nor did London's interests stop at the soon to be opened M25 motorway. The IRA leadership were fated, and a statue erected to Nelson Mandela – both now pillars of the establishment, but then regarded as dangerous terrorists. To cap it all, a giant display was erected on the side of County Hall, directly facing the Houses of Parliament, so that MP's and Peers could check the number of London unemployed on a daily basis.

None of this was cited as the main reason for abolition. It was, the Government, explained, a question of efficiency. The County Councils were an unnecessary layer of administration; such functions as were needed could be performed more cheaply and effectively elsewhere. Their resources could be used for other purposes or, better still, returned to taxpayers.

There was nothing that the GLC could do to preserve its existence, but its resources were another matter. The Council was to be abolished on 31 March 1986 – but by that time it did not intend to have many resources to distribute. If London government was going to end, it would end with a bang – literally. The reign of the GLC ended with one of the most fantastic firework parties ever seen on the Thames, bringing to a conclusion a whole year of celebratory concerts and festivals.

Getting rid of London's municipal resources proved quite a challenge. All the more so for an authority which had no responsibility for the services, such as education and health, which people cared most about. And that is where the Brunel Ducks came in.

We were delighted to help and, it soon transpired, were well qualified to do so. As the only national league team in west London, we could easily claim to be a cross borough organisation. We could certainly claim to come under the heading of recreation (which the GLC had responsibility for), rather than education (which it didn't). In fact, the idea of kids being *educated,* rather than *entertained* by our coaches was really quite worrying. Most of all, we met the criteria of being willing and able to consume public money within the required timescale.

We become part of the great GLC gold rush. I remember making a trip to County Hall one March afternoon to make sure that our grant was processed and handed over before the critical year end – no mean feat given the number of staff who were leaving in droves. I returned clutching, literally, a cheque for some £13,000 – easily the highest in the history of the club.

The GLC money was for specific purposes – mostly coaching and community activity. It was not intended, or used, simply as a subsidy to the wage bill. It did, though, allow us to build a new model of a club in which the full time players could, if they were so minded, earn more through coaching activity, and local kids were more likely to come and see their new found heroes play on a Saturday night. It was a model that survived the GLC, being maintained later by the London Boroughs Grants Unit, one of the successor bodies established by the Government when, months after deciding to abolish it, they realised what the GLC actually did.

In fact, the Brunel Basketball School, which the grant helped us establish, out lived the Ducks themselves. Strange to think that, but for Margaret Thatcher and a few boxes of chocolates, it might never have happened.

*   *   *

Unlike our chocolates, the team were not getting carried away. Triumph against Tyneside was followed immediately by pathos against Plymouth. It was another low scoring defeat against a team that had already dumped us out of the cup. Worse still, it was a team containing three of our former players. Strangely though, I didn't mind the rise of Plymouth too much. They were such a *polite* club. It is an indication of how polite they were that I can't remember the names of their Directors – by and large, you only remembered grievances. I do remember, though, that before they signed Micah they called to ask if we had any objection, and paid a good transfer fee without any argument. Likewise Ian, who they had picked up on his arrival in the South West, was at least polite enough not to play very well against us, almost grimacing with embarrassment when he scored his sole basket. In addition, they were polite enough to sign Micah's brother-in-law, probably to help him feel at home, and our record signing, Richard Parsons. In basketball terms, Plymouth didn't seem a long way from promotion. In geographical terms, however, Plymouth is a long way from anywhere. Keeping their players was to prove a real problem. Micah and his brother-in-law were to leave within three months.

The Plymouth result deflated enthusiasm, but didn't halt progress. November promised much, with five games against lower or mid table clubs, and it duly delivered five wins. Only an improved Swindon side threatened any real challenge, recovering to a too close for comfort 72–71 with a late basket in the return game. By early December, we were top of the league with eight wins from nine games, and expectations were starting to rise again.

Some patterns were starting to emerge. First, we were boring. At least, that is, to fans who liked to see the scoreboard ticking over at regular intervals.

By Christmas, no league opposition had bettered the 71 points amassed by Tyneside and Swindon. Second, success was based in depth as well as strength. We used the full squad much more than our rivals. Third, we were not the only team liable to shocks. By Christmas, we had been astounded to see Tower Hamlets overturn Tyneside and Swindon beat Calderdale, in a bazaar finish in which Calderdale had needlessly surrendered possession with two seconds left, and conceded a three point basket right on the buzzer. Calderdale also lost to Tyneside, who of course had also lost to us. Plymouth were fading, but a new rival was arriving from nowhere, or rather from Derby. They reinforced their position with a typically tense 68–62 win at Brunel. It was Derby who led the way at Christmas.

Our final league game of 1984, a win at Camden, went virtually unnoticed, although it meant that the team had remained unbeaten away from home throughout the calendar year. Amazingly, we had only played eight away games during that period, including two at Camden and one at Tower Hamlets, while we had played 18 at home. It was a very good year for cup draws, and transport costs.

All of this is background, because the conventional wisdom was that the whole promotion issue would be resolved in January. First up, on 12 January, was the visit of Calderdale for yet another home match. The following weekend we were away both to Calderdale and Tyneside. A good fortnight and we had one foot in the first division. A bad one and the excitement would be over for another year.

*   *   *

In the meantime, we decided that the players needed a diversion, while club funds naturally needed a top up. The answer was to go international. It was time for the Brunel Ducks to take on the world. We started with our usual caution. The first step in our quest to become a global brand would be Wales.

During the past year or so we had developed a good relationship with a club called Ton Pentre, nestled somewhere in the Rhonda Valley. It is a little known fact that basketball has quite a history in the valleys. Ton Pentre had won the first ever National Junior finals in 1938, beating London Polytechnic by the staggering margin of 12–6. They held the title for a record eight years, aided by the fact that it was not competed for in five of them. Then, as the English Basket Ball Association had become ever more efficient and professional, it dawned on them that Wales was, well, not England. As the main team in Wales, Ton Pentre was left with no one to play.

The club had sent a women's team to our May tournament in the past two years. They were a friendly bunch, and competitive. Now, as part of the strategy to put the club more firmly on the basketball map, they invited us down to play a promotional match. Not just one match, either. It was agreed that we would take three teams. Each would play its counterpart and the winning club would be the one not with most wins, but most points overall. Every point would count.

It was an attractive idea. As National League activity had grown, it had become difficult to maintain the idea that we were a club, with teams at several levels. This was a way of doing something together. Moreover, Ton Pentre offered to pay for the coach and promised excellent hospitality and, as long as no one found out about this, I could charge everyone a fiver for the day out, providing a welcome boost to funds over the otherwise barren Christmas period. In return, we donated the 'Ruccanor Trophy' for the winning club. Or rather, we recycled the Ruccanor Trophy, which had been donated by the now defunct Milton Keynes club for a promotional game three years previously. It was just sitting there, looking lonely in the trophy cabinet.

So a full coach load of us set off on the Sunday before Christmas. As promised, the basketball was good, but the hospitality better. By the end of the evening, totalling the three match scores became a challenge, but it was generally agreed that we had won the trophy 'by about 20 points'. Nor was it clear exactly when the end of the evening was. All attempts to leave were met with strong resistance. We began to suspect that the Welsh strategy was to kidnap us, as part of a plot to develop a national league of their own.

Two hours after the scheduled departure, we set off with huge amounts of best wishes, the Ruccanor Trophy and a vague set of directions. It was slow progress, and we sort of noticed that a disproportionate share of the travel seemed to be uphill. After a further hour, the bus stopped. We were lost. Those of us on the left hand side of the bus looked out of the window and saw, to our horror – absolutely nothing. And I mean nothing – certainly not a road, or a pathway, or anything above or immediately below us. We were on the side of a mountain, and beneath us lay a sheer drop. And such road signs as could be found were entirely in Welsh.

A committee was convened to take charge of the map, and try to plan an escape strategy. Ten minutes later, it reported back.

'The only way from here,' announced the bus driver 'is down'.

We had to agree with him. We only hoped that it wasn't an omen.

*   *   *

I am writing this account of the home game against Calderdale with the aid of the original match score sheet. Score sheets simply convey the facts of the game. This one is an exception. Drama simply oozes out of it

Everything started normally. It was a phoney war, with such scoring as there was being evenly distributed. After seven minutes, it was a measly eight points all. Then the baskets started flowing, and they were all one way – the wrong way. In the next eight minutes, Calderdale scored 21 points, Brunel a pathetic six. Normally, a 15 point deficit was not terminal, perhaps equivalent to being two down in a football match. But we were a team famous for low scoring games and defence. We had blown it.

Three minutes before half-time, we trailed by 33–20. Then, the tide turned, and we started scoring. First Dave scored, then Mike scored, then Eric scored, then Perry missed a free throw and Dave scored from the rebound, then Eric scored, then Dave scored, then Dave scored again, and again, then Phil scored, then Eric scored. This flow was interrupted by half-time, but not by Calderdale. Incredibly, we had moved straight from 20–33 to 40–33. The crowd were celebrating wildly.

They were celebrating prematurely, too. We had just seen the equivalent of a tidal wave, and tides sometimes move in both directions. Now Calderdale's tide was coming in – 17 points to our four. Calderdale led by 50–44, and we were inside the last 10 minutes. We responded with a mini tide of our own. Three successive baskets, and it was 50 all.

The next tidal wave would win it, but there were no more tidal waves to come. From now on, the teams not only traded baskets, but insults, and so did their officials. And here is another difference between basketball and football. In football, referees put up with huge quantities of abuse from managers and officials and players and are pretty powerless to do anything about it, beyond telling them to move seat and maybe suggest a future fine or suspension. In basketball, the irate referee can take immediate revenge, through the medium of the technical foul.

The great thing about technical fouls is that they are moments of high drama, and influence the course of the game right away. In football, a referee accused of being blind, biased or brainless must wait days for a half hearted apology. A basketball referee can simply turn to the bench, raise the fingers of his left hand to the palm of his right, and award two free shots to the other team, even if they are not in possession. Entire matches have been decided on the award of a technical foul.

The closing minutes of the Calderdale game saw not one, but *three* technical fouls. First, Coach Mark was enraged at a call against one of our bench players, Anton Ferris. His observations converted Calderdale possession into Calderdale free shots, which in turn put Calderdale back into the lead. But Calderdale weren't to be outdone. Three minutes later their coach incurred the official's anger. Not only that, but he earned a technical for protesting against the first technical. He was dismissed from the hall. A whole succession of free shots put Brunel five points clear. It seemed like the biggest lead for hours.

But it was not decisive. Within the last 30 seconds, a basket from none other than our former friend Jamie brought the margin back to two points. All we had to do was keep possession to record a famous victory – but somehow Calderdale's American Mark Washington grabbed the ball. The question was – exactly how? The crowd shouted foul, the diminished Calderdale bench disagreed, the officials went with the majority. The Calderdale coach, now watching from the balcony went ballistic. Perhaps fortunately, officials had no ability to penalise comments from the balcony, and in any event, the last thing that we wanted was free shots that could have been missed, giving the ball back to the opposition. So we resumed with side line ball and, this time, managed to keep it. Brunel won the most important and dramatic game that the court had ever seen by 72 points to 70.

'Fifty bloody thousand pounds a year we spend on this club – and we end up with referees like you' screamed one of the few Calderdale officials still allowed in the hall to the officials as we crowded round the scorers table. I was shocked – not at the behaviour, but the amount. It was three times more than our budget.

'Get him out of here'. The Commissioner shouted at me, having quickly reverted to my role of official match promoter and peacekeeper.

'Too right!', I replied. I didn't want our players and coaching staff hearing those kinds of figures.

*   *   *

Suddenly, we were not only promotion challengers, but front runners. It didn't change my life, and I suspected that it wouldn't last. Maybe things would have been different if we had been given time to get used to our new status. As it was, there was only a week before the weekend from hell – the return visit to Calderdale, followed right up by the Sunday afternoon encounter on Tyneside. Telling us that we were only 10 wins away from Division One was like telling your average quiz contestant that he is only 15 answers from becoming a millionaire.

There was a strange inevitability about that weekend. We didn't collapse, or self destruct. Both games were close and yet, in my heart, there wasn't a single moment when I thought that we were going to win either. At Calderdale we were never more than eight points behind, yet never seriously challenged. At Tyneside, the maximum margin was seven, the ultimate margin of defeat four. There, is of course, a much more detailed story that could be told about both games, but not in this story. This book is intended to be happy, nostalgic and record triumphs. Above all it is unashamedly biased. Readers who want the same level of detail on Calderdale's victory as ours of the previous week, will have to wait for the Calderdale club history. This is basketball, not the BBC.

Nor am I going to talk much about the Tyneside disaster – except for one incident. In basketball, the most awe inspiring, dramatic and memorable way of scoring a basket is the slam dunk. A dunk is when a player gets his hand above the level of the basket and literally slams the ball through it. A dunk can have a psychological impact on both the opposition and the crowd. A dunk can bring the house down.

Perry's dunk, three minutes from time, didn't bring the house down, but it did bring the basket down, and the whole backboard behind it. A great tactic, I thought, since even the EBBA had to accept that playing a match with only one basket wasn't exactly fair, and a game that we were not going to win would now have to be abandoned. We might even be able to claim that the facilities were faulty, and claim the points, and then there was our coach fare – could that be claimed back? There was also the hotel, meals, emotional stress, and…

Dream on! All hopes of a spectacular and unfair escape from our most important defeat of the season were ended when, miraculously, a reserve backboard, of exactly the same quality and dimensions was produced and erected, all within 10 minutes. And the matter didn't end there. Not only did our inevitable defeat become inevitable again, but I heard the Commissioner commenting fawningly to the Tyneside Chairman how glad he was the club had read rule 63 (b) of the playing regulations. He was sure, he emphasised with a degree of emphasis that made me feel somehow uncomfortable, that not *all* clubs could say the same thing.

What the hell was rule 63 (b)? Come to think of it, what were the playing regulations? I had only ever read the league regulations, and they were bad enough. I had always assumed that the playing rules were relatively simple. Five players on court at once; 20 minutes in each half; two points for a basket – that sort of thing. This was all stuff for the coach, not hard pressed club Directors. Needless to say, no one actually *had* a copy of the said regulations, but subtle enquiries confirmed that there was, indeed, a rule 63 (b), and that it did oblige National League clubs to have a reserve backboard available.

This was worrying. Not because we had been breaking a rule. We had been breaking lots of them for years. But I did pride myself on at least *knowing* the rules that we were breaking. I guess that was my, 1980s style, definition of risk management. If new rules were starting to emerge from the vaults of the basketball authorities, who knew where it would end? But worse, far worse than all of this, rectifying this problem would cost money – money which, quite naturally, we didn't have.

I tried reasoning with Chairman Mike. All the usual arguments about how much exposure and prestige Brunel was getting, how it all depended on our operating in the National League, and how these things inevitably came at a cost. He was having none of it. A new backboard of the type required would cost well into four figures, and probably never be used. The Middlesex League didn't have such a requirement. I protested that in the Middlesex League it was virtually illegal to be over five feet eight inches tall, and, if you were, to jump more than three inches off the ground, but this time, he really couldn't be convinced. The only remaining question was whether we should tell the league authorities about our omission. That, at least, was a no-brainer.

So, for the remaining years of our national league existence, I spent every home game worrying not only about the result, whether the crowd was big enough to pay the bills for the week and whether the commissioner would be happy with the sandwiches, but whether the basket was going to be brought down by a dunk. A split-second might well end our national league career. Had it done so, you would not be reading this story.

*   *   *

The immediate problem was how to put a brave face on the two defeats. The programme for our next game, at home to Tower Hamlets, shows how hard we tried. My editorial stressed that everything was still up for grabs, that all the top teams still had to play each other, that only a couple of slips on their part would put our fate back into our own hands and, most of all, that it was critical that the fans kept giving us their support (and money). All stirring stuff, but none of us really believed it. We had been given a fleeting, unexpected and probably one-off chance of the most unlikely promotion in the history of the league – and it was now gone.

The only compensating factor was that the results at least took the pressure off. The programme for the next few weeks did not look onerous, and with only one game to come against a top four club – the final at Derby – there was no reason why we should not end the season on a high. Tower Hamlets once again did us the courtesy of rolling over with out a flight, as did Nottingham, Stoke, Sandwell and Colchester. We were heading for a total of 17 or 18 wins (depending on the result of the game at Derby) from 22 games. It was by far our best record ever. Things could be worse. Perhaps we were just being greedy.

As the season meandered to this comfortable conclusion, there seemed to be less urgency in checking other results. By the last week of February, each team only had three games left, and there looked to be no prospect of the upset that would put promotion back into our grasp. I even missed our midweek game at home to Camden, having gone to York to do a week of interviews for work. I made a late night phone call to make sure that all was well. I was mildly relieved to hear of a routine win, highly satisfied to be told that a decent crowd had turned up, and absolutely delighted to be reassured that no one had brought the backboard down.

The following night, Tower Hamlets were at home to Derby. Having seen both teams play, and knowing just how predictable basketball could be, there seemed no reason to check the result. Nor was there any means to do so. There were no mobile phones, no internet and national newspapers didn't hold the press for second division basketball games that didn't end until 10 o'clock. Dick Turpin could have probably got the result from London to York faster than any means that I could think of. It was two days later, and back in the office, that I checked the EBBA bulletin to find that Tower Hamlets had pulled off the surprise of the season.

To this day, I don't know the story of that game. Maybe Tower Hamlets signed a new player for the night, or just played out of their skin. Maybe Derby was under strength for a mid week game, or their players were distracted by the thought that some local yob might be stealing chocolates from their car. Really, all I cared about was that it wasn't a misprint. It wasn't.

The result, together with other games between the 'top three' meant that Derby had now lost three games, Tyneside, Calderdale and Brunel four each. Calderdale and Tyneside both had better points difference than us, based on games between the teams concerned – but the last round of matches not only saw Brunel visit Derby, but Calderdale go to Tyneside. The two winners would be promoted.

Saturday 9 March 1985 was going to be the biggest night in the club history, and I hope that you are feeling as excited about it we were. First, though, and for reasons that will become obvious, we need to divert into a brief discussion on theories of procurement.

*   *   *

Years after this story ended, Carol wrote a dissertation on the subject of tendering and procurement. I am thus one of the few people in the world with some idea of how mind blowingly, yawningly boring the subject is. In what is described as an extensive grey literature, there seems to be a theory, model or definition for everything. Like all professionals, procurement executives are keen to persuade us that their work is both difficult and important. There are so many things to take into account – quality, fitness for purpose, continuity of supply, direct and indirect transaction costs, internal and external relationships, environmental and ethical considerations… the list seems endless.

The complexity is surprising, because sometime towards the start of this story, I had invented the Brunel Ducks definition of procurement. This is simple, easy to remember and capable of being utilised in a wide range of circumstances. It asserts that procurement is 'a means of getting things as cheaply as possible'.

We applied this definition at every opportunity. On our rare weekend trips, the strategy was to fix up accommodation at the last possible minute, assuming that this would give us the best possible price. Few people realised how close the team came to camping by the motorway in sub-zero temperatures. For the visit to Sandwell and Plymouth, earlier in the year, the Sports Centre telephone had been requisitioned to call dozens of possible guest houses and hotels in Cheltenham about 36 hours before setting off, on the assumption that they would not be packed out for a weekend in February, and desperate for our call. Did you know, by the way, that of over 80 establishments in Cheltenham bearing the name 'hotel', at least three quarters no longer actually take guests? That was true in February 1985, at least.

In the case of coach transport to away games, the Brunel Ducks definition of procurement involved a tendering process at the start of each season, on the assumption that bulk buying would reduce the cost. We went through this process three times, and on each occasion it was won by the same firm. I won't use their real name, since I think they are still in business today. In fact, I wouldn't be surprised if some of their coaches were still stranded on the same stretches of motorway where we left them over two decades ago.

Global Coaches were friendly, cooperative and cheap. Flexibility was a particular strength. Sometimes they showed up on time, sometimes a bit late. Sometimes there was a video, sometimes there wasn't. Sometimes they gave us little extras. Returning from Leicester on a freezing January night a couple of years before, a fire had broken out above the wheel. On a trip to Nottingham the following season, the windscreen had smashed. On the trip to Stoke only a few months before, they had changed the pick up time at short notice, and we had had to leave without some supporters. Overall, though, I liked them.

So, Global Coaches were accident prone, and their vehicles had a particular dislike for the Midlands. It's all very well saying that you can predict what happens next. You have the benefit of hindsight.

*   *   *

Today, the play-off game to decide promotion to the Premiership is referred to as the 'richest game in football'. It has been estimated that up to £90 million is at stake, in a single, winner-take-all showdown. In the world of basketball, our visit to Derby on 9 March 1985 was roughly equivalent to this in terms of its importance. The main difference was that the winners would receive a monetary prize of zero, and require an increased expenditure of thousands of pounds for the following season.

It was, nonetheless, the most important game in our history and probably the only chance the club would ever have to get to the first division. There was a mixture of excitement and apprehension as we set off, for the first time ever, in two full size coaches. These had been arranged, naturally, at a further discount with our friends at Global Coaches. In deference to the importance of the occasion, it had even been agreed that those players who wanted one could have a double seat all to themselves.

So we had a cheap coach and a cheaper coach. The cheap coach was for players, guests and little people who would not take up much space. The cheaper coach was for everybody else.

This arrangement turned out to be was fortuitous since, somewhere on that anonymous stretch of the M1 that is near Milton Keynes, near Northampton but not actually *at* anywhere, the cheap coach chugged to an untimely halt. I didn't think this much of a problem. If anything, it had happened so often that it might help the team feel at home, and we were, after all, in the hands of the most experienced company in England at handling coach breakdowns. I could tell from the accusing look on his face that Coach Mark didn't agree. Fortunately, at that point, cheaper coach chugged up behind, still functioning. The players got on and replaced the supporters. Some started asking about getting their money back. Now *that* was a problem.

I think that the breakdown was the turning point of the entire day. By the time that both coaches reached Derby, any tension had disappeared. Getting there was a triumph in itself, and we were on a high. In the pre-match discussion

I was asked by the commissioner whether I really thought that Brunel could survive in the first division. The answer, of course, was no, but it was a question that I was thoroughly fed up of hearing. Not only were we ready for promotion, I said, but that we had now reached a stage where we would find it much harder to survive in Division Two.

'Did you mean that?' asked Carol after the commissioner had moved on.

'No'. I mused. 'I'm just so fed up of being condescended to, I couldn't resist it. Anyway, we'll probably never get the chance to find out'.

I was wrong – we were going to find out. It was not only the biggest night in our history, but Derby's too. The 1,300 crowd was easily their biggest ever; perhaps it affected them more than it did us. Either way, Brunel established a 15 point lead. The home crowd got behind their team, pulling the deficit back to five inside the last three minutes, but given our style of play, even that was a huge margin. Then one of Derby's Americans fouled out, and that really was the end. Eric rounded things off with a terrific dunk. Two coach loads of fans were delighted. I was just relieved that he didn't try anything that spectacular at Brunel.

*   *   *

The night at Derby would have been a fitting end to the season – or indeed, to my entire basketball 'career'. However, there was still the matter of the National Trophy to resolve. Remember the National Trophy? It is the competition open to any team in England – except the good ones. The competition that we had reached the final of three years previously, but hardly troubled the scorers in before or since.

I mention our 1985 National Trophy campaign with particular pride. Whatever my limitations, I have never at any stage in this book claimed any credit for the achievements of Brunel Ducks Basketball Club on-court. Sporting honours are ultimately won by players and coaches, not administrators, and certainly not by committees. The 1985 National Trophy was, in part, an exception to this rule.

The National Trophy was not a priority for the EBBA, or for the National League committee (made up almost entirely of Division One clubs) which was responsible for it. It was no surprise, therefore, to find that the draw for the 1984-85 competition was relegated to something like agenda item 23 of a meeting in the early autumn of 1984. Nor that, after three hours of discussion almost entirely related to how big clubs were going to get bigger and leave the rest of us in the lurch, I was the only representative of a Division Two club left.

As item 23 approached, I glanced down the list of clubs entered. Whoever we were drawn against, I reasoned, progress to the final would be tough. It was already clear that the newly merged teams at Tyneside and Calderdale would start favourites, and that Derby had become established as their strongest challenger. Avoiding all three would take a miracle – or, well, perhaps not. I had not studied geography since the age of 14, but the possibilities were suddenly obvious even to me.

It was ten to five, we were the last item on the agenda, and there was no one in the room who remotely cared about anything other than heading for home. It was worth a shot. As we reached the item, I ventured the view that, in view of the increasing financial difficulties of Division Two clubs, the need to consider fans and the fact that at least one round of the National Trophy would have to be played mid-week – perhaps we should move towards a regional structure for the early rounds. Perhaps even, for all rounds until the final?

I made these comments with my head faced downwards, looking intently at the table rather than my dwindling audience. Even so, I couldn't help catching a glance at the duty EBBA official, who had the brief to stay with us until we were safely off the premises. He was open mouthed – this was sheer hypocrisy, even by basketball standards. For five years, every time some condescending pratt from a big club had suggested that little leagues like ours should go regional, I had been the first to object. Despite the cost, playing at national level was the thing that separated us from the other teams in our region. In any event, our transport was cheap – in more ways than one.

I waited for the response, whether in the form of reasoned opposition or ridicule. Had it come, I would write the whole suggestion off as a joke – shrugging my shoulders, grinning and saying something like 'well, you can't blame me for trying'. But there was no response. The big clubs really couldn't care less whether the National Trophy had a regional basis, or for that matter whether there *was* a National Trophy. As for EBBA, they probably feared that I was about to launch into another long diatribe about unnecessary costs. And, of course, it was almost opening time at the bar – a milestone more significant than it would be today, since, despite her supposed desire to de-regulate everything, it took Margaret Thatcher until 1988 to give us the freedom to drink beer in the afternoons.

The hastily conducted draw gave us a path to the final which would involve games against Colchester, Camden and Plymouth. As an added bonus, we would even have the home draw if we made it to the final. It wasn't the first time that a league meeting had produced such a blatantly unfair conclusion, but it was the first and only time that I was responsible or, felt so smugly satisfied with it.

These finely tuned political skills were not appreciated by the team, who seemed determined to wander away from their carefully laid path to the final at every opportunity. Each of their Trophy performances was way, way, below normal standard. Against Colchester, they threw away a winning lead and only progressed after extra-time. Victory against Camden only came only came after overcoming a 13 point half-time deficit. The semi-final at Plymouth would have gone into extra-time, too, had a last second shot from their American guard not bounced out after hitting the rim. It was as though God had made a very rare trip into the murky world of basketball, was telling me that He would let me off this time, but that in no circumstances should I ever pull a stunt like that again.

Eventually, I discounted the divine retribution theory. Had God really glanced into the world of English basketball, He would have found so much more to take revenge on than me. The likely response would have been nearer to 40 days of torrential rain than one uncomfortable afternoon at Plymouth. Also, if God had really wanted that final shot to hit the basket, then it would have done. For all the trials and tribulations, the plan had worked. We made it to the final.

Waiting for us there were Tyneside. I was pleased about this, because, unlike Calderdale or Derby, they would have nothing to 'prove' – if anything, we would want to show that we should have been champions, rather than them. In fact, we only failed to be champions by half a basket. We had beaten them by three in the league game at Brunel, they had won by four in Newcastle – the difference being two free throws conceded in desperation, right on the final buzzer.

The Trophy final summed up the season. We were behind for most of a low scoring game. Just seven seconds remained when we clawed ourselves into the lead, by a single point. Even then there was time for a last second shot by Tyneside's England international Curtis Xavier to hit the ring and bounce out, to be grabbed by a grateful Perry. We had not only won, but we had got our point back – precisely.

THE FOOTBALL CLUB

Surviving in the top division would not be easy. We grasped this point right away. By the time that the (now functioning) coach from Derby had passed Leicester, we had decided to convene an emergency Board meeting for the following Monday evening. This was a revealing insight into club mentality. Losing – either matches or money – had never been thought important enough for an emergency meeting. Winning sent us into panic mode.

Aided by three bottles of champagne (provided by Will in his personal capacity, rather than becoming another drain on club funds), the Board quickly established three options. The first was to simply tell EBBA that we didn't want to go up. The second was to try and sell the club, or at least attract investment from parties able to compete at the new level. The third was to plough on as before, in the hope that something would turn up.

The first alternative was quickly discarded. This was not so much because I had spent three years in National League meetings arguing that the incentive of promotion was critical to clubs like ours. Breathtaking U turns were so commonplace in basketball that the hypocrisy would have gone unnoticed. Instead, it reflected a feeling that acceptance that this was as far as we could go would effectively mean the end of the club. We thought it unlikely that players, spectators or sponsors could be motivated if our sole ambition was to win (and presumably decline) promotion again. The cases of Nottingham and Camden, both of whom had won Division Two in the late 1970s and either been denied, or declined promotion, and gradually gone down hill ever since, supported this view. Moreover, the circumstances of our promotion seemed so bizarre that the prospects of our ever having the opportunity again were pretty remote.

The question of whether we were the right people to grasp the opportunity was more difficult. As a Division Two backwater, it had been relatively easy to hide our deficiencies because no one cared enough. Division One, we flattered ourselves, would put us in the full glare of the media. People would actively start comparing our administration and facilities against other clubs and, more alarmingly, league rules. Players would need to be paid proper wages. Sponsors would need to be serviced professionally, or at least expect someone to pick up the phone during office hours. Even this was assuming that there were sponsors to attract. The heady days when it was assumed that membership of Division One would bring significant resources through group marketing had long gone, as had the weekly live game on Channel Four.

It seemed unlikely that any investor would want to buy *our* club. Our experience of the abortive takeover discussions just two or three years previously was that any new owners would quickly want to move the team elsewhere – possibly out of the region completely. Moreover, none of us had any idea of how to go about selling a basketball team, or who might buy one. Even by the standards of the 1980s, the idea that the club could be sold as an 'investment' seemed fanciful. Attempting to sell would also take time – and we already had less than six months to become competitive.

Ploughing on regardless also had its risks, but as the evening wore on these didn't seem so different from those that we had embarked on five years previously, without the faintest idea of what we were letting ourselves in for. The worst that could happen, we reckoned, was that we would simply lose every game, that our fans would desert us as the season progressed, and even that we wouldn't be able to pay the full time players. We would have given it our best shot, however, and for one season at least, Brunel would play against the very best teams in England. But that was worst case scenario. The more positive view, which gained credence as the evening wore on, was that something would turn up, just as it always had done. We owed it to ourselves to go for it.

That, at least, was how the world looked just after 11 o'clock on the evening of Monday 11 March 1985, after three bottles of champagne.

*   *   *

Meetings of Division One clubs were different from those in the second division. Division Two chairmen were keen to show that they were ambitious and efficient. Division One Chairmen wanted to demonstrate that they were rich. For Division Two Chairmen, running a basketball club was a major part of their lives. For those in the upper division, it was projected as part of a wider portfolio of activities, and a pretty irritating one at that.

Then, there was the football club. Rumours were rife that real football teams, keen to diversify from one loss making business to another, were about to invest heavily in basketball. Many, we were told, wanted to follow the model of continental giants such as Real Madrid, Barcelona and Inter Milan, who typically had basketball, volleyball or handball teams. No one was certain how far this process would go. Southampton were thought to be taking a stake in the Solent franchise. At least one league meeting was hosted at Villa Park, assumed to be a certain indication of interest from the Villa Chairman, Doug Ellis, in the Birmingham club. As Derby, with sponsorship from BPCC, moved nearer to promotion, it was thought inevitable that the Maxwell family would take a stake. These were, by common consensus, just the sort of people that basketball needed.

Three firm connections with football were already established. Kingston was chaired by Dennis Roach, a leading football agent. Portsmouth had been taken over by John Deacon, millionaire builder and owner of the town's football club. Most famously of all, Manchester United had taken over a club, and branded it with its own name.

Today, it seems remarkable that a global operation such as Manchester United should have any interest in owning a semi-professional basketball club, playing in a stadium that could barely hold 2,000 spectators. These were very different times. In 1989 the Edwards family accepted a bid of as little of £20 million for its controlling interest in the football club – indeed a potential new owner was presented to the crowd at Old Trafford. The club was also starved of success – having not been English champions for almost two decades. It was said that when the basketball team, having won their first national title, were paraded around Old Trafford at half-time of a football league match, the announcer not only had to explain who they were, but what they were carrying. It was a trophy.

The football representatives appeared personable, and keen to find out who we all were. When they found out they quickly decided that it was we (and not they) that were in the wrong place. In particular, it was the 'football' club that had inherited from Basketball Marketing Limited the mantles of thinking big and centralised marketing. These were now to be achieved through the creation of a 'Premier League'.

Smaller clubs – of which we the extreme version – had no place in this world, and there was little that we could do to pretend otherwise. Our defence, rather, was that this was the wrong world for basketball to be in. Since this time, the creation of a Premier League has made British football a global brand. Even had we known this, we would have argued that basketball was fundamentally different. However well marketed, there was no prospect of the English game receiving such international recognition, television coverage had not been an unqualified success and there was hardly a club in the country that could accommodate more than 3,000 spectators. Rather than major expansion, the need was for a period of stability, and greater equality between the clubs. As *Basketball Monthly* had pointed out four years previously, however, the overwhelming desire of clubs was not to enhance the product as a whole, but to win trophies in the short term.

We were cast in the role of the corner shop in the way of a major town centre development. The brave new world planned by the developers promised much, but its sustainability was untested, and in the meantime much of value would be swept away. But all of that was for the long-term. A more immediate concern was to produce a first division team within six months.

*   *   *

The role of overseas players was changing. In 1979 it was assumed that the maximum two 'Americans' were essential, and that if all else failed they could be relied on to score a high proportion of the points. By 1985, two good American players were no longer sufficient. This was increasingly the case in Division Two, but much more so in Division One where, in addition to attracting squads of home grown talent, the leading clubs had scoured the world for players with 'dual nationality'. These would qualify to play alongside the two 'overseas', players, or better still, players who had learned the game overseas and had full British nationality.

Virtually all Division One clubs had at least the one 'dual national' now permitted by league rules. Compared with 'overseas' players, these were in relatively short supply, aware of their value and often of variable quality. In fact, we only knew of one possibility.

The story of Julio Politi is worthy of a book on its own. As his name, looks, temperament and passport suggested, Julio was unashamedly Argentinian. It was as an Argentinean that he had met his future wife, Linda, who were living in Buenos Aries in the early 1980s. The timing could hardly have been worse. In March 1982, Argentina famously occupied the disputed British overseas territory of the Falkland Islands. Britain determined to regain the Islands by invasion. Britain and Argentina were at war.

Once again, the paths of the Thatcher government and the Brunel Ducks had unintentionally crossed. Linda and her family were withdrawn from Argentina, for reasons that the whole world could understand. The whole world, that is, except for Julio. He was outraged that such a thing as a minor war should come between him and Linda. Weeks later, unannounced, he came to England to sort things out personally.

Not too many Argentineans came to Britain in the spring of 1982. Those that did were not welcomed with open arms. It took time to convince the immigration authorities that pursuing a girl friend was a legitimate reason for breaking all kinds of diplomatic protocols. Still, the determination could not fail to impress. Having made the effort, marriage was almost bound to follow. It quickly had done.

The question was, had it followed swiftly enough? Linda and Julio were married in the summer of 1982. Three years later, given all kinds of good behaviour and bureaucracy, Julio would be able to apply for dual nationality. In the meantime, he had played National League Basketball as an overseas player for Camden. We knew his talents well – even with Julio as their sole overseas player Camden had been hard to beat. They were perhaps less evident to first division clubs, although Crystal Palace were rumoured to have brokered an arrangement that he would join them once his dual nationality was confirmed. Whether or not such an arrangement existed, signing Julio would be difficult.

'How much would a player like that cost?' asked Chairman Mike, at one of our increasingly regular Board meetings, which in the absence of champagne were also becoming increasingly gloomy

'Mmmm. Maybe five to ten thousand?', I speculated. I hadn't given the matter much thought. It seemed a pretty academic question.

'Not to mention salary', added Will helpfully.

'Bloody hell, it'd be cheaper to buy the whole club'.

Amazingly, Chairman Mike was right. Camden had been one of the strongest teams in the early years of Divisions Two, largely based on local and unpaid

English talent. As paid players became more prominent, Camden was left behind. Not only had they started to slip down the league, but their court, administration and attitude had started to annoy the English Basket Ball Association. So we had at least one thing in common.

Camden did have some things going for them, though. Geographically, they were in a good area brimming with local talent. The few administrators that they had were refreshingly honest, open and friendly. Unusually, the club had no illusions about their position. When, in the previous season, Calderdale asked opponents to predict the likely outcome of their matches there for the match programme, they got the following replies:

'It should be a great game, but we've got a good squad and are pretty confident' – Tyneside.

'We know we're in for a tough ride, but we'll give it all we've got' – Brunel.

'Calderdale sound good. We'll get stuffed.' – Camden.

And, they had Julio, too. If basketball had had a long term, there would have been good strategic reasons for a merger. But few basketball clubs had the luxury of looking long-term, and in the short term the advantage was huge.

Only in basketball could the value of an entire club be seen as less than that of one of its players. Only in basketball could you even think of merging with a team just to gain one player. Only in basketball would the idea even get a second glance from the authorities. Well, this *was* basketball, so the idea deserved a shot.

For a game that had rules about everything from the organisation of the toss up before the game, to the number of sandwiches after it, merging two clubs proved amazingly easy. For once, being an EBBA 'problem club' worked to our advantage. The way they looked at it, both Brunel and Camden were thorns in the side of the professional image that they were trying to portray. If nothing could be done to get rid of us both, then eliminating one of us at least represented progress.

A single phone call to Leeds established that a merger would be possible, that the merged club would retain the Ducks' place in Division One and, most of, that we would retain the registrations of all the players of both clubs. Who could object? Certainly not Camden, who were happy with the offer of a new name – the Brunel and Camden Ducks, representation on the Board and two home games per year at the nearby Sobel Sports Centre in Islington. Not the

EBBA, for whom the prospect of getting at least two games away from Brunel was an additional bonus. Not Julio, who seemed amazingly unconcerned about who he played for, as long as he was finally able to make some money from the game. Not the other Division One clubs – who regarded our whole presence as a temporary irrelevance. Even Crystal Palace, if indeed they had ever maintained an expectation of signing Julio, made nothing more than a polite enquiry. The deal was sorted by the end of June.

*   *   *

We had assumed that Coach Mark, having always entertained the ambition of operating in the National League Division Two, would be even more enthused by the prospect of a spell in Division One. At the same time Mark assumed that a Division One team would have an increased budget. Both assumptions turned out to be wildly optimistic.

For weeks, we both avoided the subject of budget. Mark, perhaps, because he assumed that we were hatching big plans that we couldn't yet reveal, us precisely because we weren't, so that there was nothing to say. It was May when he broached the issue, and even then only in a conversation in a school car park following a local tournament that we had been watching.

There was no animosity in the conversation. I reminded him that there was no extra money that would come as of right to first division clubs, promised that such increases as we did attract would be available to the team, but that no guarantees could be given. Mark disclosed that he had been approached by an ambitious, and well funded, team from Brixton that had just been admitted to the second division, and would have to weigh up his options. The outcome was that he became the third coach in as many seasons to leave the club – the first with no coaching job to go to, the second to return to junior basketball, the third to drop down to the division that we had spent all of the previous season getting out of. Staff retention was not really our thing.

So Mark went to Brixton, and I started pounding the streets of Uxbridge with increased vigour. Both of us found that we had exaggerated our positions. The streets of Brixton did not turn out to be paved with gold, while the streets of Uxbridge proved surprisingly lucrative. Strange as it seemed to its student population, Uxbridge was a boom town in the 1980s. Close to London, without the costs, close to Heathrow, for the new breed of executives who formed the advance guard of the global economy, close to the countryside, for those who wanted to get away from it all, but not too far away.

Not that relaxation was fashionable in the 1980s. After several weeks of trying to see the Marketing Director of the Allied Irish Bank, one of several companies to have located its UK headquarters to Uxbridge, I was surprised to be offered an appointment at 7.30am, smugly reassured when my host didn't turn up until 15 minutes late, and absolutely gobsmacked when he entered the room with an apology, offering the explanation that 'my previous meeting over ran'.

Whether Declan of the Allied Irish Bank did have a previous meeting I will never know. What I do know is that well before my normal breakfast time I had obtained a match sponsorship worth the better part of a thousand pounds, and that Allied Irish were not the only newly established new arrival keen to build local links. The schedule of match sponsors started to fill rapidly. We even had our first ever team sponsor. C and L Leisure was the brainchild of an Indian businessman who had decided to build a country club in Northolt. Perhaps he was new to Britain, or at least the geography of it, because to most of us Northolt seemed a pretty unlikely destination for a country club and sure enough, every time we went there it was empty. Sponsoring the Ducks was the obvious way to fill it up. Whether it worked, I don't know, but as I write C and L Leisure still seems to operate in the same location, having outlived the Ducks by over two decades. Maybe we should have sponsored them.

*   *   *

The coach problem was quickly resolved. Late in the previous season we had been approached by Dave Titmuss, former coach and owner of Hemel and instigator/perpetrator/innocent bystander/victim (delete according to taste) of the early rounds of the saga of Hertfordshire basketball described above. Dave presented himself as a refugee, basketball mad and with no team to coach or watch over. Moreover, it seemed that he was a relatively prosperous one, having retained control of the lottery which he had established in the early days of Hemel, and which had funded the club. There were other candidates, but given our financial position a candidate who had (a) first division experience; (b) did not require paying and (c) ran a basketball development lottery looked a pretty good bet. It was a no brainer.

That said, we quickly agreed that the lottery would have no relationship with the club. From Coach Dave's point of view, this was a baby that he and his wife had carefully nurtured over many years. From ours, we knew too little about its objectives, operation and finances to even contemplate involvement. There was no direct contribution to the club, although the junior team that it had helped to build played some of their games at Brunel. At an early stage, too, Dave announced that he had persuaded Martin Walters – younger brother of Nigel, and regarded by many as a better player, who had not played National League since the annual Hemel/Watford fall out of 1984, to join us, and that 'he would take care of any finances'. I had no idea what these finances were, and I didn't want to know. This seemed like the kind of coach that we could do business with.

Only four years previously, recruiting full-time American players had seemed like a luxury, to be undertaken only if we could afford it. Now it was a necessity, whether we could afford it or not. Old mentalities died hard, though, and some felt the our existing players – in particular Perry – were under rated. Free from any emotional attachment, Dave went for players that he had seen at first hand. Dale had played in Ireland the previous year; Brian with a well known touring side called 'Athletes in Action'. We were back up to the salary levels to which we had over committed three years previously, but in the circumstances, reflected that it could have been much worse.

Another part of Coach Dave's master plan seemed more problematic. Not content with our efforts over Julio, he had made contact with an 'English' American, Tony Watson, who was currently playing with Solent, still in Division One. English Americans were even more valuable than dual nationals, because there were absolutely no limits on their numbers. Or, it seemed to me, their salaries. What was worse, Tony was still registered with Solent, so there would be a transfer fee to pay. Coach Dave assured me, however, that he had 'taken care of this'. By this, he meant that he had spoken to Solent, and the fee would be only £5,000. Since £5,000 would have paid for just about our entire salary bill in the previous season, this didn't make me feel much better. We discussed it a Board meeting, and, without any idea of how either transfer fee or salary would actually be paid, agreed that he should come for a trial.

*   *   *

At this point fate, in the form of Carol, intervened. Aware that we had not had a holiday since our trip to America (much of which had been spent watching, talking and arguing about basketball) she arbitrarily booked a two week holiday in Malta for the first two weeks of September. It was intended to provide a complete break from the stress of basketball before the onslaught of the new season, and in other circumstances would have done just that. As at was, leaving things in such a state of uncertainty just led me to fret.

Making an international phone call from Malta in 1985 was not easy. These had to be booked a day in advance, at a specific time and a cost that represented a significant part of the average holiday budget. To my further disgust, there were no special arrangements for newly recruited holders of 400 British Telecom shares. By the end of the first week, however, Carol could see that, far from being a luxury, this was a necessity if we were to enjoy any relaxation at all. We blew two days spending money on a call, and fortunately found Coach Dave at the other end.

'Hi, Dave. How's it going?'

'Who's that? I can hardly hear a thing.'

'It's John. Just thought I'd call to see if there have been any developments.'

'I thought you were on holiday.'

'I *am* on holiday, Dave, and this call is costing me a fortune. So let's make it quick. What's going on?'

'Oh, not much really. Everything's fine.'

'What d'yer mean, not much?! What happened about Tony Watson?'

'Oh, Tony! I'd completely forgotten. He came to a couple of sessions, but didn't look that fit. So we decided not to go ahead.'

'Phew!!! Or rather, sorry to hear that, Dave. But I guess you're in the best position to judge, and we still have a pretty decent squad.'

'Oh, I've got some good news there. I've signed Fred Ancedi.'

'Who the *hell* is Fred Ancedi?' I almost shouted down the phone. I had visions of some expensive Italian superstar absorbing our newly acquired saving, of money that we didn't actually have in the first place.

'You know Fred and Ceddy. Fred Skeplehorn and Cedric Fredrick.

Fortunately, I did know of Fred and Ceddy, otherwise I would have assumed that he had simply made them up. Fred had played against us for several years at Colchester, Ceddy was part of the squad during Dave's time at Hemel. Both were experienced and big – 6ft 11in and 6ft 6in respectively. I could see that they would be valuable additions, but this was nonetheless a cause for suspicion. A few further exchanges were needed to establish that they were both keen to join, there were no transfer fees involved, and that their expenses were not prohibitive.

My relief was palpable. In fact so relaxed was I that halfway through the second week I finally asked Carol to marry me. I reckoned that, as a commitment, it was rather greater than that which we had just made to Fred Ancedi, but less than the one that we had narrowly avoided making to Tony Watson. It was also designed to last more than one season, and it did. Looking back, and with apologies to Fred Ancedi, it was probably the best decision of the week.

*   *   *

These developments kept us busy over the summer, but did little to improve our image among our first division peers. From their perspective, we had started as underdogs who should never have been promoted in the first place, had only been able to recruit a dual national player by merging with his entire club, acquired the preposterous title of C and L Leisure Brunel and Camden Ducks, and had an English strike force led by guys called Fred Skeplehorn and Cedric Fredrick. In my wilder moments, I could see why we were not taken entirely seriously.

Added to this, we started the season exactly where we left off the previous one – at the side of the motorway. Befitting out new found status as a first division club, it was a rather more modern and fashionable motorway – the M23 to Brighton rather than the tacky old M1 to Derby, but somehow no one seemed to appreciate this when our bus broke down after just 20 miles. A fleet of taxis got us to Worthing, and a respectable enough defeat to established first division opposition in the first round of the National Cup. Our first league game had also ended in a clear, but respectable loss to the Champions, Kingston.

Elsewhere in this book, basketball has been described as more predictable than other sports. That holds for perhaps nine out of 10 games, but it is not a universal truth. The week that followed provided ample evidence for this.

Sunday 22 September was horrible. There is just no other way to describe it. It was our first home game of the new era but, being out of term time at Brunel, was one of the two fixtures that we had agreed to play at Islington. The opponents were Hemel, a 'lower half' team that we needed to run close if we were to have any prospect of staying in the division. We didn't. In fact we were nowhere near, fell further and further behind and ultimately lost by the horrific margin of 36 points. Worse still, the squad got more and more dispirited. I wondered whether some of them would stick the season out. We were acutely aware of how badly things could go wrong – we need look no further than Sandwell and Liverpool, both promoted in a blaze of optimism but not surviving to tell the tale, as warnings. In the meantime, there was nothing to be done but to go home and count the gate revenue on the living room floor. Even then we got lost and, being a new venue, the receipts were less than usual. It was a very bad day.

Sunday 29 September was fantastic. We were away to Sunderland, who had faded a little since being National champions in 1981, but were still regarded as a solid mid table club. Our team was unchanged, with one exception – Julio's nationality had been cleared. This in itself put everyone in a better frame of mind, and boy did they show it. Ten points behind early on, we edged in front by the interval, but the critical period was shortly afterwards, when Sunderland had simply no answer to a full court press. Suddenly we were 20 points in front. We won by 15. Best of all, it wasn't just Julio that made the difference – it was a genuine team effort. One of the key elements in the second half effort had been Dave Emanuel, widely regarded as one of our bench players who had joined during the close season. Our last contact with Dave had been as one of the seven dwarfs from Milton Keynes against whom we had set a new league record three years before.

Precisely because basketball *is* predictable, and because it is such a close knit community, it is no exaggeration to say that this was a result that shook the basketball world. I know that from the number of phone calls that I took in the next 24 hours; I can't imagine what Coach Dave's phone must have been like. The official line, of course, was that we had always been confident in the team, and that it had been the Hemel result that was the exception. Dave had the credibility – and maybe even the belief – to pull that off. Hiding my relief was more difficult. For me, this win had made us a *real* first division team. Yeeeesssss!

*   *   *

1985–86 was my favourite season in basketball. This wasn't because of the quality of the games, the venues, or the attention that we were getting, and it certainly wasn't because we were dealing with more friendly or genuine people. Rather, it was because every game was a new adventure. We were in a league where we shouldn't be, playing against teams and people who regarded us an irrelevance, and changing their – and our – expectations almost by the week. More than anything, it was the pure *cheek* of what we were doing that appealed to me.

The adventures flew thick and fast. The following Saturday was the glamour match against Manchester United, our first home game at Brunel. I had wanted this game early because, quite frankly, it was a chance to get at least one capacity crowd through the door before any decline set in. I needn't have worried. The Sunderland game might have been only one win, but the team were on a high. We led by 10 at half-time, were just one adrift going into the last minute, and eventually lost by five. The crowd loved it. But the really great thing was how disappointed everyone was. We had taken on one of the best three teams in English basketball, lost in the very last minute, and we were actually *disappointed*.

Our next target was a home win. Our chance came in a Wednesday night game against the 1984 National Champions, Solent, whose last league appearance at Brunel had resulted in our biggest ever defeat. As with that occasion five years previously, we tried to dampen expectations in the pre-match publicity, all the more so since Dale was injured. But these were extraordinary times. Inside the last minute, we crept in front by a single point. Then we regained possession with 10 seconds to go. All we had to do was keep it. In their desperation to get the ball back, Solent committed a foul with just one second remaining.

One second can mean more in basketball than any other team sport in the world. In basketball, the ball does not come into play when it leaves the player putting it into court. The clock does not start until it is touched by another player. This was one rule familiar to a whole generation of armchair British fans, for whom the 1972 Olympic final, delayed for some long-forgotten reason and shown live late on a Saturday evening when all other events had finished, was the only live basketball they had ever seen. That game was famously stolen by

Russia after regaining possession with three seconds on the clock and hurling it the full length of the court to be tipped in for the winning basket.

The rule was familiar to Solent, too, and their subsequent tactics enraged an already buoyant crowd. Every time the ball was thrown in, Solent committed a foul before it could be touched by another player. Thus, it was back to the side line for another Brunel ball, with the same second obstinately remaining on the clock. To some, this seemed a petty pointless tactic to simply keep the game alive, but the cause was not hopeless. With arms and bodies flying everywhere as players jostled for position, there was every chance that the referee would see a Brunel foul instead. There was the possibility that Brunel would be tempted to the free throw line, rather than taking yet another sideline ball, with the possibility of at least one shot being missed and Solent regaining possession. There was also the possibility that, under pressure, Brunel would crack and simply pass the ball to a Solent player.

This process was repeated three times. The crowd, anxious both to celebrate a historic win, and do so in time for their lectures the following morning, were not happy. Then, on the fourth attempt, something strange happened. The ball was played in to be followed, almost simultaneously, not by two but three noises. There was the unmistakable slap of hand on body which signalled yet another foul, and the shrill, if weary sound of the referee's whistle. Both were drowned out by the deep blast of the match hooter. Somebody had got fed up, and the precious second had disappeared.

The somebody – or rather some *bodies* concerned – were Ann and Mike – our scorers, whose responsibilities included turning the electronic clock on and off. Appointing the scorers was the responsibility of the home team, and although Ann and Mike had no association with the club, they had been doing the job throughout our national league career. Solent were livid. How, they demanded, could the second disappear if the foul had been committed before the ball was properly in play? All attention turned to the Commissioner, who sat next to the scorers and had the power to over rule, and put the clock back, if need be.

There followed an impassioned debate about the nature of time. It would have graced the average university common room, let alone an undergraduate physics seminar. It was explained to the Commissioner that the speed of light was faster than the speed of sound. Thus it was quite possible that the scorers had *seen* the ball enter play before hearing the referee's whistle. Possible, too, that the referee's whistle was a fraction late – remember, that it was this, not the foul, that the scorers had to respond to. Finally, the fact that a second remained on the clock did not necessarily mean that a *full* second was remaining, because these things were rounded. It was quite possible that, although Solent thought they had a full second, in practice they had only, say, 0.6. I had never been more proud of Brunel's history as a technological university.

My contribution was less scientific. It was all very well, I pointed out, to debate the finer points of physics, but in real life there were now a couple of hundred people on the court, who assumed that the game was over. If the Commissioner had noticed anything wrong, he should have said so right way. Restarting the game now would be impossible and, I declared in my most pompous voice, I could not guarantee the safety of those involved. It was, we all agreed, a fait accompli.

My only remaining concern was that the integrity of Ann and Mike, regarded by everyone who knew them as completely honest, had fleetingly been called into question. This, I reckoned, needed to be sorted out once and for all.

'Peter, you didn't think seriously about restoring that last second, did you?' I asked our friendly local Commissioner.

'Not really. When you've been in basketball as long as I have, you've seen just about everything.'

'Thanks. I was just a bit concerned about Ann and Mike. It would be terrible if their conduct were called into question. I'd want that to be completely clear.'

'Well, I don't think it's worth putting in my match report. What could I say?

'You could tell the league from me that if Ann and Mike were corruptible, we would have bribed them years ago. They would certainly have had complaints about it before now.'

'That's fair enough. Everyone will believe that'.

*   *   *

Normally, I avoided the club office on the day after a game. There was usually a lot of mess to clear up, a smattering of complaints and, in any event, I needed to re-establish a presence in my day job. The day after the Solent game, I made an exception. It was our first home win in the big time, a proper working day and I wanted to bask in the glory.

On this particular Thursday, we did a brisk trade. Not only had the result provided another jolt to the basketball world, but the game ended in such chaos that quite a few people called to check the course of events, and to send congratulations. Plenty more came in to buy tickets. Complaints were at a minimum, perhaps because everything had been said already.

In the midst of this, I took a call from Linda, Julio's wife. I didn't know Linda well, but she seemed to be very pleasant, even tempered and sensible. As we exchanged greetings, I couldn't help feeling that she was leading up to something. For a horrible moment, I thought that it might be win bonuses. Then the conversation took a surprising turn.

'John, can you remind me of the final score last night.'

'How could I forget? It was 75-74.'

'Well, that's what I thought. And, well, we did *win*, didn't we?'

'Linda – you were there! Of course we won!'

'Yes, well I *thought* so. But people are saying that we lost.'

'Trust me, we didn't. Who on earth is saying that?'

'It's here, in the newspaper. *Brunel Ducks 75, Solent Stars 76*'.

'They're always getting things wrong. What bloody newspaper?'

'Well, that's just it. It's not any newspaper. It's *The Times*'.

Thus it was that, in another contribution to the development of the 1980s, the Brunel Ducks helped point out to one small corner of the English middle class a trend that had been developing some time. *The Times,* once the pillar of the British establishment, whose word could be trusted on everything from matters of State to attendance at society weddings, had finally lost its place as the fountain of all wisdom.

FORTRESS BRUNEL

It was the Manchester United finish, rather than the Solent one, that set the pattern for our early homes games. Against Birmingham and Manchester Giants, we competed well, got in front, only to lose by a narrow margin in the final minute or so. The same happened in a British Masters game against Crystal Palace, although we cared less about that. The British Masters was a new innovation, introduced partly to provide more games and revenue, partly to incorporate Scottish clubs. Extra games against League One teams would have been ideal for us as a second division club – we had already played Colchester, Tower Hamlets and Brixton in the group stages. But we were now trying to be a big club with a small and, apart from Dale and Brian, part-time squad. Added to all this, it was the Colchester game where Dale had picked up his injury.

Not that all extra games were unwelcome. In early November I took a phone call from Coach Dave, who nonchalantly asked whether it would be possible to organise a game against the full England squad later in the month, prior to their departing for a critical World Cup qualifier against Israel at Wembley. The only problem was that, since the Israel game was on the Thursday, the game would have to be on a Monday.

Brunel versus England! Just think of that, both for prestige and money! Mike wasn't a man for sudden spontaneous gestures, however, and agreed that we could have the court only if I squared the arrangement with the badminton club, who normally used it on Monday nights. If ever there was a reminder of our roots, this was it. Fortunately the badminton club were as amenable as ever. In fact one of the permanent legacies about my time with the Ducks was how reasonable and *nice* badminton players are. The game went ahead with a packed crowd and, guess what, ended in another close defeat. We did, however, do better that Uxbridge FC who several years earlier had played the England football squad as training for an international match. I believe that they lost 11-0; we only lost by 10.

Everyone was frustrated by the close defeats, but I didn't mind too much. I was just pleased that we were being competitive, and as long as the games were close, the crowds would keep coming. It might even make them more determined to see us win, as my first ever basketball match watching Doncaster against Crystal Palace a decade previously had done for me. It was also important to have realistic targets, and our aim had always been to keep out of the bottom two. It was becoming clear that our main rivals in this regard were Bolton and Tyneside, and our visit to Bolton in November produced an invaluable third victory. It was a comfortable one, too, with every member of the team getting on the score sheet.

*   *   *

I was disappointed that there would be no opportunity to play Doncaster who, for financial reasons, had been forced to drop out of the First Division. In their absence, I guess the team that I most dreamt of us beating was Crystal Palace, the bad guys in that fatal first ever experience of basketball. Although not the force they once were, Crystal Palace were still the biggest name in English basketball. There were plenty of teams that we could expect to beat before them.

Nonetheless, holding them to three points in the British Masters was an encouragement, and their visit for a league game in early December was eagerly awaited. The game followed a familiar pattern, with Ducks opening a first half lead of 11, only for Palace to gradually claw back to take the lead with four minutes left. I couldn't help but feel that we had read this particular script before.

This time, there was a difference. The Palace fight back had come at the expense of too many fouls. American Tom Seaman was on four fouls after eight minutes; England international Mike Bett fouled out after 15; American Buba Jennings and coach Jim Guyman conceded technical fouls with two minutes to go; Jennings fouled out seconds later. One outcome of this was lots of free shots for the Ducks. There were nine in the last three minutes, and all were converted – the last four by Phil. Steve Ball, the only player to have played for both clubs, had a long range shot on the buzzer to win it for Palace, but was polite enough to miss.

Brunel and Camden Ducks 102, Crystal Palace 101. I read the result over and over again, as well as the increasing volume of press reports that we were now collecting. The Ducks were no longer the exclusive property of the *Uxbridge Gazette* and *Radio Hillingdon Hospital*. In a full match report in the *Guardian*, Bob Pryce described us as 'perennial overachievers from an obscure part of suburbia'. We were becoming famous.

Dramatic wins over the likes of Crystal Palace and Solent were all very well, I told myself, but the real aim was *still* to keep out of the bottom two. In this context, our visit to Tyneside, one of the few sides below us in the table, the following week would be much more important. So important, in fact, that Carol drove us all the way there in her mini, after we had failed to meet the team bus on the motorway. It was a tale of her works Christmas party at Felixstowe, too much carrot whisky and too late a breakfast. I expect that you can imagine the details.

Five hundred miles in a mini is a long way at any time. After this particular 40 minutes of basketball, it seemed much too far. Everything had begun well. Starting as favourites for the first time all season, Phil rolled off four successive baskets to establish an 11 point lead within the first eight minutes. Tyneside pulled level by half-time, but it didn't seem to matter. With 10 minutes to go we were 12 in front again, before disaster struck.

One of the alluring features of basketball is that every foul counts. After committing five personal fouls a player is excluded from the game. In practice, this influences the thinking of the coach much earlier than that. If an important player commits a third foul say, in the first half, he would typically be substituted to avoid the risk of a rash fourth foul, or at very least his defensive game would be restricted.

At Tyneside, the foul count was vital. Shortly after half-time, both Dale and Brian were on four fouls. Five minutes into the second half, Dale was on five fouls and off. As the game progressed, Fred, Martin and Julio moved onto four fouls also. With nine minutes to go, Brian also fouled out. We were 12 points up, but two players down, and three more on the brink of being so. We were holding on for dear life.

We only scored nine points in the final seven minutes, but by slowing the game down there was still a chance that we might not be caught. With five minutes to go, the margin was eight, two minutes from time it was down to one, but we pulled away again. Inside the last 30 seconds the lead was three, but Tyneside scored and drew a foul in the process. The resulting free throw drew them level in the nick of time.

Having spent the last 10 minutes grimly, and unsuccessfully, hanging on to the lead, no one gave us much chance in extra-time. Extra-time is five minutes. By the third we were losing by five points. Had we not been 250 miles from home and dependent on Carol's mini to get us back, I might have left early. It was just as well that I didn't. Four successive baskets in two minutes reversed the whole tide of the previous half hour. We won by a single point.

*   *   *

Financially, our venture into the big time was going surprisingly well. We had been cautious in our estimate of home crowds, being aware that, while Brunel versus Manchester United on the first Saturday of term was a sure fire sell out, it would only take two or three big defeats for enthusiasm to wane. Close defeats, however, were not in the same category. The games were exciting in themselves, and the fans were just keener and keener that we would win one day. The England game, too, had been a financial bonus.

I was always concerned, though, by the 'Miscellaneous Income' line in our budget. We always included several hundred pounds under this heading on the assumption that, as Mr Mcawber put it, 'something would turn up'. It usually had, but in dribs and drabs. This year, we enjoyed a windfall from a very surprising source.

In football, if a team reaches the semi-finals of the FA Cup, then the League game that it is due to play on the same weekend is automatically re-scheduled. The same principle applies in rugby, cricket and any other sport run by sane individuals. Not so in basketball. Twenty years previously, when there had been no central administration, it had been deemed the responsibility of the team concerned to contact their opponents, and cancel the match. Curiously, the rule had never been changed.

This technically had been of little interest to the Ducks, having won precisely one National Cup tie in their history. Nor did it seem likely to be so this time, since we had once again been dumped out at the first hurdle. It gradually dawned on us, though, that it might apply to Portsmouth, our scheduled opponents for Cup semi-final weekend.

Portsmouth – now under football ownership, were a very different team from the poor, friendly and reassuringly unambitious club from the same town that we had encountered in Division Two. This team had not obtained its place in the top league through anything as mundane as winning promotion, but by taking over the franchise of a team already in the First Division. They looked in every sense to be a highly professional outfit.

The irony is that, while the friendly, affable and unambitious Portsmouth of two years previously would almost certainly have known the rules about Cup semi-finals, business like, professional and ambitious present day Portsmouth did not.

We were scheduled to host Portsmouth on the evening of Saturday 14 December – not a great date for us, since the Brunel term had just finished, but an even worse one for Portsmouth, whose National Cup semi-final was scheduled for Birmingham the following afternoon. As November turned into December, we expected a phone call to ask us to cancel. The call never came.

Any decent, reasonable person putting the interests of basketball above the narrow interests of their own club, would naturally have called Portsmouth and drawn this to their attention. We didn't, of course. Basketball affected your entire morality. We reasoned that, if the game went ahead, we would be facing a Portsmouth team with one eye on a much bigger fixture the following day. If it didn't, we would be in line for some compensation. In the meantime, we would sit tight and do nothing.

The first that Portsmouth heard about the problem was evidently in the week of the fixture itself, when the official league bulletin was issued. They evidently went ballistic, not unreasonably citing the problem as another example of the amateurish way in which basketball was run. The league called me, just in case we had already assumed that the game was off. I expressed complete astonishment. I had assumed, I said, that Portsmouth wanted to play us on their way to Birmingham. Everyone in the sport seemed to regard us as an irrelevance – why would Portsmouth be any different? This sounded disturbingly credible to the authorities. For once, the rules were on our side.

On the following Wednesday evening, my home telephone rang. Carol rushed in in a state of high excitement to say that it was the Chairman of Portsmouth Football Club, calling from his private box. John Deacon was affable enough, but wanting to concentrate on an important League

Cup fourth round second reply against Spurs, which he was watching live, doubtless with important business associates. I was watching Coronation Street and eating my tea, so we both wanted to conclude our business quickly.

Within the duration of the television advertisements we established that (a) we would agree to cancel the game (b) Portsmouth would compensate us for the lost revenue and goodwill (c) that it was really all the fault of the EEBA and (d) that Portsmouth were leading Tottenham by 1-0. Both of us put the phone down happy. We had effectively gained revenue worth another home game, and moved the new game to a more convenient date in term time. Portsmouth had got an irritating little club out of their hair – at least for the moment.

*   *   *

We went into the Christmas break with five wins under our belt, which was at least four more than most people expected, and almost certainly enough to avoid relegation. An unspectacular home win over Tyneside in the first game of 1986 cleared even my lingering doubts. Now, it seemed, we could enjoy the rest of the season without pressure.

The narrow home defeats that had characterised the first two months of the season had not unduly concerned me. If anything, I was relived that teams such as Manchester United, Birmingham and Manchester Giants were not completely demolishing us. What none of us could have known, at the time of the eight points defeat to the Giants on 16 November, was that this would be our last league defeat at Brunel for 15 months – a total of 14 straight wins. This was the age of 'Fortress Brunel'.

It was hard to see why Brunel was so impenetrable to first division opponents. This wasn't so in the Second Division. Our 62 wins before promotion had been almost equally divided between home and away games. Then again, in the Second Division there was not a huge difference between Brunel and some of the other venues where we had played. In the First Division, there certainly was. I knew this from the trickle of complaints that arrived in the office on the Monday and Tuesday following each home game.

First division clubs had different expectations. Their players did not expect to have to mingle with the fans to get into the court, but we only had one entrance. They didn't expect to have to warm up to a children's song written to accompany cartoon ducks marching along. They didn't expect to have home fans shouting in their ear from a distance of about 18 inches when they went to take a sideline ball. Even their supporters had expectations, like comfortable seats and programmes with staples.

There was a fine dividing line between the natural advantage enjoyed by a home team, and the unfair advantage created by breaking the rules. As the run of unlikely home wins developed, the English Basket Ball Association started to take an unhealthy interest in which side of that dividing line we were on. Sometimes, it was difficult even for us to say.

Readers of my age will remember the famous Morecambe and Wise Christmas shows. My favourite was the one in which their guests included Andre Previn, leader of the London Philharmonic Orchestra. There is a famous scene in which, frustrated by Morecambe's piano playing ruining his performance, the composer eventually squared up to him.

'Is anything wrong?' asked Morecambe.

'Only' said Previn, through clenched teeth, 'that you are playing the wrong notes'.

'I am playing the *right* notes'…, responded Morecambe in his most pompous and deliberate tone.

…'But not necessarily in the right order'.

Our attitude to the rules was a bit like Eric Morecambe's approach to playing the piano. We *did* observe the rules – but not necessarily in the right order or, for that matter, all at the same time. For example, there was a minimum capacity requirement and rules about the amount of space between the edge of the court and the seating. We could do one, but not both. So, when we were not expecting a capacity crowd, we ignored the capacity rule and allowed a comfortable margin between the court and seats. If there were tickets to be sold, then the seats would appear again. The capacity requirement would be met, but the relationship between the crowd and players would be, as we liked to describe it, intimate.

This was not simply a question of comfort. In basketball, a ball is not deemed to be out of play until it has actually bounced. It was common for players to make spectacular dives into the crowd in order to scoop a ball back into play. On big match nights at Brunel, this was an option only open to the home team. An away player would invariably find that the ball had already been caught by a seemingly apologetic student. There was little that the match officials could do but restart with a Brunel side line ball.

*   *   *

The idea of Fortress Brunel was particularly evident in the rearranged home game against Portsmouth. Postponing the game from immediately before Christmas had seemed like a good idea at the time. As the rearranged date in early February drew near, I was beginning to wonder. We would be below strength. I found to my horror that, with typical enthusiasm, Phil had scoured the fixture list at the start of the season to find a gap for a skiing holiday. The rearranged date meant that, in our 139th competitive game at national level, we would be without him for the first time.

Portsmouth, by contrast, were on a roll. They had become established as the team most likely to challenge the dominance enjoyed by Kingston and Manchester United, and their role as a model for the basketball arm of a football club was attracting lots of attention. Publicity in a national newspaper a few days before the game showed just how far they had come in terms of professionalism. One of their players, Colin Irish, was reported to be earning some £40,000 per year. It was not a lot by the standards of sporting superstars, even in 1986, but huge by the standards of a sport which hardly ever attracted a crowd of more than three thousand.

It was also, as I spluttered indignantly on reading the article, almost twice as much as our entire budget for the year – players, equipment and dodgy coaches to away games included. Somehow, the comment stuck. Whether the rumour was true I have no idea, but by the evening of the game the entire crowd were convinced that one Portsmouth player was being paid more than the entire Brunel budget. It just wasn't *fair*.

The torrent of abuse that resulted from all quarters did not seem to affect Colin Irish, who defiantly started the game with a three point basket, but as time progressed, it did influence the game. It was a turning point in the season. Up until this point, the onus had been on Brunel to demonstrate that their place in the first division was justified. On this particular night, the burden of proof passed to the big guys. Our place was safe. Now it was for Portsmouth, and their highly paid players in particular, to justify their place in the order of things.

It was as though both teams knew that something wider was at stake. It was a game of barnstorming pace and intensity. The six point lead that Portsmouth established in the first minute was the biggest margin of a first half in which the lead changed hands nine times. At half-time the teams were locked at 54 all. Neither coach wanted to risk substitutions. Only 13 players entered the court in the whole game – seven from Brunel, six from Portsmouth.

Something had to give in the second half, and it wasn't going to be Fortress Brunel. Three minutes into the second half, the lead changed hands for the 11th time, giving Brunel a single point lead. This time, they were not going to let go. There was no single turning point, but with three minutes to go we miraculously led by 13. Dale just seemed to score basket after basket – seven in a row. On the other side of the score sheet, a notable absentee was Colin Irish – who contributed just one basket and three fouls during the first 18 minutes of the half. In the last two minutes, both Portsmouth and their star player recovered, but not quickly enough. Our 104-100 win was our biggest scalp yet.

* * *

Every single game in the first two months of 1986 was an adventure. Had they taken place at any other time in this book, each would have merited two or three paragraphs. As it is, they just merged into a dreamlike fantasy in which it seemed that just nothing could go wrong. At home, we were invincible. On our travels, there was a resounding fight back against Hemel, which gained ample revenge for that early season drubbing. Julio hit a staggering seven three point baskets in that game, and followed up with a further five in a first ever win at Manchester Giants. Even the defeats had a touch of heroism about them. Against Manchester United we were ahead with just eight seconds to go before losing by just one point. Maybe we were getting greedy.

For two months, everyone in the limited community that was basketball wanted to know how a group of players who, apart from Dale and Brian, had been around the lower reaches of the league for years were suddenly taking the first division by storm. Come to think of it, so did I. Had the English Basket Ball Association thought of drug tests in those days, we would have been randomly selected every week.

Maybe one factor was the lack of pressure. Having got past five or six wins, there was no prospect of relegation. The season was therefore defined as a success by early January. Every additional win reinforced this. Equally, there was no possibility of progressing beyond our comfortable lower mid table position to the end of season play-offs, which were confined to the top eight clubs.

Or was there? There were 15 teams in the league, so to make the top eight a team needed to broadly win as many games as they lost. By mid January, our record comprised eight wins and 13 losses. Wins over Hemel, Manchester Giants and Bracknell took us to the heady levels of 11 and 13, but it was the 12th win against Portsmouth that transformed everyone's aspirations. There were now three games left, including two at fortress Brunel. A routine win over Bolton, and we were just one game away from qualification.

How can I describe the importance of reaching the National League Championship Play-offs in 1986? Can you imagine how modern day teams in the football Premiership feel about clinching a top four place, and qualification for the European Champions League in the following season? Good. Well – qualifying for the basketball play-offs was nothing remotely like that. Reaching the lower reaches of the Play-offs entitled a team to extend its season by playing a single series of games against a higher ranked team. In the unlikely event of victory, it then entitled the bearer to a further two week wait before playing in the final four play-offs at Wembley. Four weeks extra cost, virtually no extra revenue. Reaching the play-offs, in my opinion, was not only getting beyond our station as a basketball team, but the height of irresponsibility from a financial point of view.

Enter, with their usual immaculate sense of timing, the English Basket Ball Association. On the morning of our final home game – a Wednesday night encounter with Worthing – there arrived the weekly league bulletin. This contained the staggering news that, after counting up available sponsorship, it had been decided that teams qualifying for the play-offs would receive a one-off bonus payment of – wait for it – £750.

I doubt whether this announcement caused much excitement in the wider basketball community. In fact I doubt whether the likes of Kingston, Portsmouth or Manchester United even noticed it. Well, I certainly did. Years of arguments over kit numbers, court sizes and office accommodation had taught me to scrutinise the league bulletin for any sign of new regulation that needed to be observed – or more likely avoided. Here, at last, was an announcement that might actually benefit us. Seven hundred and fifty pounds, together with a bumper gate for the additional game, would just about cover the costs of our rash excursion into the upper reaches of the league. Not only might we qualify, we might even be able to afford it.

The players were blissfully unaware of this potential transformation of our club finances, and most would have been completely uninterested had they been told. From the nerves in the opening stages, however, you would think that they had suddenly been offered a win bonus extending into the millions. Absolutely nothing went right for the first half. It took us seven minutes to get into double figures; it was nine minutes before a foul decision went our way, after 19 minutes were we 13 points behind, when Dave Yewman achieved the doubtful distinction of fouling out before half-time. Three successive baskets in the last minute reduced the margin to seven at the interval, but both the game and the precious cheque for £750 were in peril.

If nothing went right in the first half, virtually nothing went wrong in the second. We were ahead within eight minutes, kept our noses in front for another six, and the final six were a triumphant procession, as the visitors were outscored by 25 points to 9. We lost the last game, but our place in the top eight was secure. In fact we finished seventh. A big mistake, as it turned out, since this qualified us to play Kingston – second in the league but very much the form team, in the play-offs.

There were no fairy tales in the play-offs. We fought bravely in the first game at Brunel but never quite looked like winning. In the return at Kingston, we almost took the tie into an unlikely deciding game by levelling the scores at 121 all in the last minute, but it was not to be. The champions were not pushed as hard in either of their games at Wembley.

We didn't win the play-offs, but there were plenty of other accolades. Dale and Brian were both selected for the league 'all star' team; Dave was named 'coach of the year', and in a reward for my three years patient membership of the Hillingdon Sports Advisory Committee, the club was named Hillingdon's 'Team of the Year', which unlike the more prestigious EBBA awards, actually produced some cash – a cheque for £300 from a local double glazing firm. The combination of the sponsorship deal and that fact that I was on the committee led to all kinds of jokes about the clarity and transparency of the decision – but no one really doubted that it was deserved.

For the third year in a row, things had turned out better – much, much better – than we had any right to expect. In the Britain of the 1980s, such achievements were not a cause for concern, but something to be latched on to and exploited to their full potential. The history of the stock market in 1986 and 1987 provides ample evidence of a belief that the laws of gravity no longer existed. I was not so sure.

THE BEST OF TIMES
- THE WORST OF TIMES

In the early days of our National League adventure, I knew most of our regular supporters by sight. Not only their names, but intimate personal details such as their regularity of attendance, whether they were entitled to a discount and the likelihood of their buying a match programme, draw ticket and can of Cola at half-time.

Promotion, bigger crowds and the fact that I no longer lived on the campus had changed all this. Now, even some of the regular supporters were just familiar faces. It was, though, good for the ego when they recognised me.

One such occasion came on a sunny afternoon in June 2006. It was outside Uxbridge tube station, and I was returning home after an exhausting day of research, so it was probably about half past three. My serine progress was interrupted by a vaguely familiar face, which had recognised me and wanted to say how much he had enjoyed the season. 'I really hope' he said 'that we can do it again'.

These words stuck in my mind. There was no talk of going further, building on success or even keeping up the progress that had been made. 'Do it again' said something quite different. These could have been the words of an occasional friend with whom one had just spent a mildly enjoyable evening in the pub. A one off evening, which one vaguely hoped might be repeated – sometime.

The words were apt. In basketball, however successful a season had been, there was always a need to start over again. Not quite from scratch, since you inherited a squad of players and some awareness among the fans and sponsors, but to retain the players they needed to be paid, and without them the fans and sponsors might well disappear. And the resources to pay the players would have just about been cleaned out by the end of the season. They had to be raised all over again.

This was fine when things were on an even keel, because generally speaking if something had been possible last year, then it would probably be possible next year. Over achievement, though, was a serious complication. It was not possible to over achieve year after year, and the cost of trying could be catastrophic. Ask Coventry, Southampton, Bradford or any of the other teams that succeeded in hanging around in the Football Premiership for too long, only to suffer serious financial problems when gravity belatedly took effect.

We had also had the now traditional setback of losing our coach. This time, at least, the reasons were credible. Coach Dave had made no secret of his desire to move on to greater things eventually; we had just not realised how soon eventually might be. His award as 'coach of the year', together with the general lack of English coaches in Division One, had made him a strong choice to coach the national side. At least, this time, we had a coach who was leaving to move forward. The previous three had left us, respectively, to return to playing, coach in junior basketball and coach in the division that we had just left.

The fact remained that the best we could hope for was to keep the players that had served us so well, and hope that they could once again over perform, without the element of surprise that had served us so well in our first season. Even if they did, they would merit higher salaries, and the options for coaches who did not require payment were running out. The hardy annual fund raising activities of a sports festival, three tournaments and umpteen sacks of teddies were starting to look woefully inadequate.

*　　*　　*

There was also the issue of a wedding to contend with. In retrospect, getting married was a significant development. At the time it seemed less so. Despite the frenzied attempts of my parents, prospective wife and in laws to get everything organised, somehow an event that seemed months away always ranked lower in my priorities than a basketball game the following weekend.

For a start, I failed to realise that getting married outside either of our home parishes required a special certificate. This problem was resolved only by an emergency visit to an archaic office near Westminster Abbey and handing over £40. My eventual stag night comprised four people (one friend, one friend who arrived late, one girl and me) and was over by 11 o'clock. My hair cut depended on how fast the queue moved at my local barbers on the morning of the service. And, if you believe the front page of the *Walton Herald,* of the following Thursday, I even forgot to get a best man.

The last bit is untrue. I did not *forget* to get a best man. Nor, contrary to widespread belief, did I not have enough friends to produce a best man. In fact I had a reserve best man. What I didn't have, between the two of them, was a *competent* best man. Perhaps, like the Royal family, they should have been required to travel separately, but that is being wise after the event. As it was, both best man and reserve best man stopped on the way to the service to get some cigarettes, returning to find that everyone had left and they had no map to guide them. It could have happened to anybody, although it was perhaps 20% more likely to happen to Eddie and Mark than most. I also had a contingency plan. Never, at any time, had I surrendered control of the ring.

Surprisingly, given the level of chaos, basketball didn't play a large part in the wedding day. The guest list was a rare reminder that there was once a time when we both had friends outside basketball, and even relatives. The basketball connection was confined to a handful of players, and to the former teacher who had been responsible for taking me to that first fateful game 11 years before, and who was invited as a punishment. Niall, who had been so reliable in destroying the evidence of Larry Sheldon's charge on the referee three years earlier, was naturally invited to take the wedding video. Carol and I were both acutely aware that his experience of wiping evidence might turn out to be useful in future.

There was to be no escape from basketball, even for the day. The Silvermere Hotel and Golf Club, carefully selected by my wife and in laws for its complete isolation from all things basketball, turned out to be a regular haunt of the Crystal Palace Team Manager, Mike Stapleton. It wasn't a huge breach of security. Mike had seen former Coach Roy at a distance following his round and wandered in to see what was going on. Our conversation was brief – we agreed that we had been lucky with the weather, that both of our teams were broke and that, as far as we were concerned, if the new season were delayed until Christmas it would still be too soon. We joked that perhaps, between us, we had enough money to put out one team. In fact, it was a pretty typical conversation between everyday basketball folk, but one that was to have important consequences.

*   *   *

The honeymoon was uneventful from a basketball point of view. Perhaps this was because it was earlier in the summer than the ill-fated Malta holiday of the previous year. Perhaps it was because it was, well, a honeymoon. As the three weeks came to a close, however, the realisation dawned that on my return there would be just six weeks before our first fixture. I was increasingly anxious about what would be waiting on my return.

In fact, among the pile of letters and messages that had been stacked up by Stuart, our latest youth trainee, two stood out. The first was a letter from HM Customs and Excise, informing us that we had been selected for a VAT inspection. The second was a series of messages from Crystal Palace Basketball Club, asking if I could call on my return.

The VAT inspection really cheesed me off. Value Added Tax, for the benefit of our overseas readers, is a sales tax. It is levied on the final customer of a product – in our case spectators, sponsors and advertisers, collected by the business and sent off to the authorities, net of any tax that could be reclaimed, quarterly. VAT was increasingly important during the 1980s because the Thatcher government preferred taxes that were less visible and applied to everyone, rather than taxes that came straight from your pay packet and mostly affected rich people. Before coming to power they had vehemently denied clams that they would double the VAT rate. They promptly increased it from 8% to 15%. Aren't politicians *clever*?

What made it worse was that we had registered for VAT voluntarily. The previous autumn, we had realised that a £5,000 transfer fee for Tony Watson would attract £750 VAT, which we could re-claim if registered. Although the deal had not gone through, there was no turning back. Even though our turnover was below the threshold for compulsory registration, we were paying over a little chunk of our hard earned revenue to the taxman. In my opinion, Her Majesty's Government should have been bloody grateful.

The only consolation had come in the summer period. For our first three quarters of registration, we had dutifully dispatched cheques for several hundred pounds, usually on the last day possible. During our fourth quarter, we were out of season and had no revenue, but we had used a telephone and other items that were subject to VAT. I gleefully sent off a return (on the first day possible) to inform Her Majesty that Her government owed us Thirty Two Pounds and

Fourteen Pence. Her Majesty's representative did not see the funny side of this, and had decided that we had an 'irregular' pattern of activities, which merited further investigation. There was, I screamed down the phone, nothing in the least irregular about a sports club that only played at certain times of the year, but it was all to no avail.

Ironically, VAT was one area where we had been completely scrupulous. I can't think why, because the opportunities to shave pounds from the gate money, virtually all of which came in cash, or lose the occasional invoice from the file have been well known to small businesses for decades. Maybe we were getting too old and respectable. Either way, it wasn't the fear of being caught with our hands in the till that made me angry, it was the amount of time that the inspection would take, and the sheer cheek of it.

The inspection was scheduled for a Wednesday afternoon. Carol (Company Treasurer) took an afternoon off work and I (Club Director) yet another break from my studies. We tidied the club office to present a 'poor but efficient' look. Every file, every paper was in place, and ready for inspection. Even the bears promised to be on their best behaviour

This was not, however, the way that VAT inspections worked. My telephone call had not persuaded the authorities to abandon the visit, but it had convinced them that we were a ramshackle little organisation not capable of defrauding the government of anything important even if we tried. This opinion was reflected in the choice of inspector – a recent university graduate on just her second assignment, keen to impress and much more nervous than we were.

Sarah (we were soon on first name terms) was quite frank about all this. The visit, she enthused, was more about 'establishing a relationship' than investigating individual transactions. Of course, she needed to ensure that we understood the main principles of VAT, but most of all, she wanted to understand our organisation and business. She was here to help.

I didn't believe a word of it, but as we walked around the building (to 'get a feel of the environment in which we operate'), even I was finding it difficult to ascribe a hidden purpose behind some of the questions being asked

'So how many players are there in a basketball team?'

'Well, 10 in total, but only five at once. And we don't pay them all. And those that we do are not subject to VAT – are they?'

'No, of course not! And this is the hall where you play games?'

'Yep.'

'Wow! How many spectators can you fit in?'

'Almost a thousand, but it's a real crush. We're not usually full. I've got the full attendance figures in the file here...'

'Oh, yeah! And I saw as I came in that you have a turnstile?'

'Well, the building does. But we've never used it. It's too far away from the court and we don't have access to Reception on game nights. But we do give the crowd tickets so we can be sure exactly how many are here. Here's an example...'

'What? Oh! That's fine. You can't be absolutely precise, we understand that. 'Is that a sauna? Is that part of your operation too?'

'It's part of the Sports Centre – but that's separate from the basketball club. The players don't use it. Well, if they do they pay for it themselves. It's nothing to do with us, and there should be no tax...'

'No, of course not! I just thought I might book a session for myself. And you have squash courts, too...?'

The exchanges went on for the best part of two hours. Sarah had clearly passed her course in how to 'put clients at ease', with flying colours. All attempts to look at specific numbers, transactions or papers were brushed aside. The problem was that these particular clients had not anticipated being put at ease for two hours, and had other jobs to go to. We were wondering how to bring things to any kind of conclusion, when Dale, our American star recently returned from his summer break, wandered in.

It was hard to imagine any two people less alike that Dale and Sarah. Dale was 6ft 10in, black American and a man of very few words. Sarah was 5ft 2in, white, English and with an abundance of them.

'Who's this?' – a typical minimalist greeting from Dale.

'Dale! This is Sarah, she's a tax inspector. She's come to look at our accounts. If she finds anything wrong, we may not be able to pay you this week...'

'Oh, I'm sure there won't be,' gushed Sarah. 'I was just explaining to Carol and John that I'm really here to establish a general...'

'There ain't better not be,' interrupted Dale.

Dale's appearance at least provided evidence that we were a real basketball team, with real basketball players. Sarah seemed quite impressed by this. The meeting ended shortly afterwards, and as far as I can recall the only actual number that she took away with her was that of Dale's telephone.

To my great surprise, a letter arrived from HM Customs and Excise two weeks later. It confirmed that the inspection had all been in order, but that following a detailed analysis it had been agreed that our definition of advertising and sponsorship during the year had been too broad. In view of this, it had been agreed that we were entitled to a refund of about £50. It was all there in black and white, precisely detailed.

We never saw Sarah again, and I doubt whether Dale did. She is probably now a senior official, saving millions of pounds for Her Majesty by interrogating large multi-national companies about their tax affairs in minute detail. In case she is, I should say that I am completely unable to remember her real name.

*   *   *

It took me some days to respond to the call from Crystal Palace. I hadn't taken it as seriously as that message from the VAT office. Clubs were always calling each other with spurious enquiries about players, mutual moans about the EBBA or just casual gossip. I hadn't realised how much until we had started to pay our own phone bills.

When I did, I was astonished to find that the casual discussion at our wedding about having one good team between us had raised a few eyebrows. Palace, it appeared, were going through a very bad patch. Of course they would have a team to put out at the start of the season, but whether it would be competitive would be a different matter. Perhaps we had a lot in common. Perhaps we should talk further. Perhaps I'd like to meet their Chairman, Alex Falk, over dinner at *Simpson's on the Strand* on the following Thursday?

My first reaction was that the Brunel Ducks and Crystal Palace had absolutely *nothing* in common. Whether in good times or in bad, everything about that club was on a completely different scale to ours. In good times, they had attracted major benefactors and sponsorship. They had done more to put British basketball on the international map than any other club, before and probably since. In bad times, they were very bad. Palace were not the sort of club whose Directors would spend their Sunday lunchtimes sticking up posters in local pubs, or match days delivering discount leaflets to local residents. They did not seem to be the sort of people who would scour local business for £75 programme adverts, or who would man stalls at local carnivals. In short, times at Crystal Palace were either very good, or very bad, with very little in between. Now, they were very bad. At least one limited company had already been wound up.

I briefly considered a thesis comparing the decline of Crystal Palace with a Marxist interpretation of British society. They were the aristocracy, once brimming with money, who knew how to spend it with style, and give themselves real status. In recent years, they had found themselves challenged by the rather vulgar 'new rich', the likes of Harry Smith, Dennis Roach and John Deacon, who had made their fortunes through 'trade', and were asserting that their money was every bit as valuable as that of the old aristocracy. Now, they were also being challenged by the peasants (us), who had little money and even less style, but worked hard and were starting to claim political rights. Perhaps automatic promotion and relegation was the equivalent to the universal franchise? It was all much more interesting than my real thesis.

In the Marxist view of basketball we, or at least our class, would ultimately come out on top. But that was the long-term. In the short-term, our position looked pretty vulnerable too. We had a little money in the bank, as always after the summer fund raising programme, but it would not be enough to see us through a whole season. In the previous season just about everything that could have gone right, did go right, and we had still just about broken even. That would not happen again, and we had no margin for error. It seemed to me that if Marx wanted to defend his position, he had better get down here and start selling lottery tickets. Otherwise I preferred the approach of the economist John Maynard Keynes, that – 'in the long term, we are all dead'.

So I did go to meet Alex Falk. I had never dined at Simpson's before, and didn't like it. It seemed a place of faded grandeur, pompus and bloated, which had been somewhere really special in the past, but now wasn't and did not know quite how to react. It was all so appropriate.

On the other hand, I did like Alex Falk. I had never met him before, and his role at Palace had not been a very high profile one, at least in the basketball community. He struck me as a forthright, hard nosed and successful businessman, who like so many others was genuinely bemused by the fact that simple business principles just didn't seem to work in sport. He had probably become involved in basketball for the reason that most business people become involved in sport. He had been persuaded by enthusiasts that here was a challenge that would be interesting in the short-term, and offer glory and recognition in the longer term. In the good times, Crystal Palace had done all of this. But the good times were over and he did not have the time, or possibly inclination, to work out why, and what could be done about it. From what he could see, consolidation was a possible way forward, and London's two premier clubs working together could only be a step in the right direction.

The more I thought about it, a merger with Crystal Palace was not the outlandish proposal that it first seemed, but the easy and practical option. I thought about my conversation with the supporter outside Uxbridge tube station, about how in basketball everything had to start again every year. I thought about whether it was really likely that we could match the achievements of the previous year, let alone move forward with our current resources. I thought about the implications of going backwards – very few clubs had been relegated and survived to tell the tale. It was possible that Brunel Ducks could have survived for years as a small club in Division Two, but that strategy had failed both Nottingham and Camden and, in any event, we were now past the point of no return.

We discussed the matter as a Board – still very much including the Camden representative Phil Hayfield. The dominant feeling was not one of scepticism, or even excitement, but one of relief. None of us had ever thought of giving up our careers for basketball. I was the nearest to doing so, but then again I didn't really have another career *to* give up. Running a team at this level was starting to threaten even this. Moreover, for the first time, we had reached a point where there seemed to be no way forward. We were, as Bob Pryce had written in the *Guardian* following our win over Crystal Palace the previous year 'perennial overachievers'.

There were, of course, lots of details to sort out. Both clubs had supporters, traditions and egos to satisfy. We recognised that the provenance of Crystal Palace would be useful in its own right. But the economics of the situation, as well as our own preferences, required that the merger should be rather more 'Brunel' than 'Crystal Palace'. It was agreed that all but four league games would be staged at Brunel, the team was largely based on the Ducks squad of the previous year and four out of the seven Directors were appointed from Brunel. We had a new name – BCP London, reflecting Brunel and Crystal Palace as the component parts, and a new company was formed. Years later the encyclopaedic *Pawprint* basketball web site included the new squad as a continuation of Brunel in its all time league table. As a result, we retain to this day the status of being one of the 30 or so most successful teams in the entire history of British basketball, despite not having thrown a ball in anger for the last 25 years.

Two other groups needed to be considered. The first was the English Basket Ball Association. This was a much more significant merger than the one involving Camden a year previously, and closer to the start of the season. It was possible that there would be objections, and we took this seriously enough for Roy (representing Palace) and I to attend a meeting in Leeds to explain. In fact the response was much the same as the previous year. It was disruptive but inevitable, and, as with the Camden arrangement, it would at least rid them of one troublesome club. I was beginning to realise that it wasn't just us that the EBBA didn't like. They didn't really like anybody.

The second was the players. This was not as big a problem as it seemed, since two of our main squad from the previous year – Fred Skeplehorn and Martin Walters – had already indicated that they wouldn't make it this time round. The merger was expected to produce two front line players from Palace – England internationals Paul Stimpson and Mike Bett, so it wasn't as though large numbers would be cut. But it did seem to me, at least as a courtesy, that I ought to have a word with Phil. It was possible that, as the only player to have been with us since the start of our adventure, he might feel that his role, or that of the club, was being diluted. To assure him that it hadn't, I suggested that we meet in the *Royal Oak* in Harrow Town Centre, which in keeping with club tradition was just about the least fashionable pub in the district. If anything could convince him that the new style Brunel would be as mean, unfashionable and penny pinching as ever, this was it.

Our discussion was overdue – probably by about seven years. I had tended to avoid discussions with players – partly because I had no technical knowledge, partly because I didn't want to clash with our succession of coaches and partly because they always seemed to be asking for something. Phil, it turned out, had taken a similar line with administrators. He had only the vaguest idea of who ran, financed and owned the club, and frankly didn't really care. He just liked playing basketball. The questions that he asked were practical ones – where would the games be, what about training, who would still be playing? Even the fact that we might be able to pay him something, for the first time ever, was a subsidiary concern. He was still happy to play.

So we were ready to go places, and the first place we were going to was Hemel Hempstead.

*   *   *

One advantage of merging so late in the summer was that it gave us the choice of two fixture lists. The EBBA had been persuaded that we should take over the Brunel list, on the principle that the majority of home games were being played at Brunel, and it would mean less disruption. In reality, principles were nothing to do with it. The Brunel list gave us a quieter, and rather easier start to the season than the Palace one. After the initial game at Hemel, there was a two week break before the next fixture, which we had negotiated to coincide with the start of term.

This was important for two reasons. First, the new squad was stronger than that of either club in the previous season, but had never actually played together. Getting them to do so effectively was the job of the Coach. Ah, yes, that was the second reason. We didn't have a Coach, either.

We were engaged in a race against time. By popular consensus, the addition of two leading English players to a settled squad that had reached seventh position in the league in the previous season ought to have made us, say, the fourth or fifth best team in the country. But it would take time for the team to blend together, and no one was obviously in charge of that blending. One journalist wryly commented that we could not have had an easier opening to the season if we had selected our own fixture list (which, of course, we had), but I was not so sure.

The Hemel game was going to be hard on the nerves. Less than a year previously, they had trounced us by such a margin that most people concluded that were hopelessly out of place in the top division. Now they were the underdogs, relishing the opportunity to catch a highly ranked team off guard. Defeat would not put our merger at risk, but it would lead a lot of people to question what, in reality, we had gained from it, and leave us open to much ridicule.

Thankfully, it didn't come to that. Brian was thrust into the role of player coach for the first time, and looked uncomfortable. So did most of the players. But it was a scrappy game on both sides. Fascinating for the basketball tacticians, but much less inspiring for the spectators. We scraped home by nine points.

*　　*　　*

The Hemel game taught me nothing about basketball, but it taught me a lot about myself. In fact, it is no exaggeration to say that Wednesday September 24th 1986 was a defining date in helping me to realise what really motivated me in life, and, more particularly, why I had spent almost a quarter of it caught in the obsession that was basketball.

I didn't understand basketball. I didn't even like it. I didn't, I realised shortly after the final hooter, even like winning that much. Or at least, I didn't like winning just for the sake of it. It suddenly struck me that the key thing was not winning, but winning against the odds – the sheer check of putting one over bigger and more powerful opponents. It was the one thing that had unified my life to date. In my environmental campaigning, in joining the Labour Party, in supporting Rotherham United and a Yorkshire Cricket team that stubbornly refused to include players born outside the county borders. Maybe even in choosing to study at Brunel in the first place.

It was also the one thing that had been missing at Hemel. Hemel was our 77th league victory to date. Most of the previous 76 had been unexpected or at least highly uncertain. Even those that we had been expected to win were part of a wider plan that was itself against the odds. This one was different. We had been expected to win, and we were expected to do well all season. So what?

*　　*　　*

The two weeks following Hemel gave players and management time to re-group, even to get to know each other. This all went as well as could have been expected. The different philosophies of Brunel and Crystal Palace basketball clubs were there for all to see. Crystal Palace loved spending money, Brunel hated it. In good times, where there was money to spend this would have caused tension. These were not good times, financially, for either club.

So we were drawn together, if not by friendship, at least by acceptance that we were working in the same direction. The key people at Crystal Palace were more human than their reputation in the sport had suggested. Terry was a florist who looked like a bouncer and reasoned like the type of common sense bloke that you could share a drink with in any good pub on a Friday night. David was an accountant turned advertising agency owner who, as we were to find, could take on a wide range of roles. Ed was a car salesman who looked and spoke like a car salesman. There were no problems with the two new players, either. Paul, England captain and ultimate diplomat, made a point of strolling into our ramshackle office before the first training session to say how much he had heard about the way we ran the club, and how much he was looking forward to working with us. These two statements were quite incompatible, of course, but the thought was appreciated.

We quickly solved the coach problem. Brian had showed every prospect of being a leader, and had huge support from the team. Before the end of the Hemel game, though, it was clear that he wasn't comfortable in the role of player coach, and all persuasion to get him to change his mind failed. To our surprise, David – one of the Palace 'gang of three' offered to take the role on. He had coached the highly successful Crystal Palace women's team for several years – and we were grateful. Most of all, as I realised when he showed up for his first session in a perfectly formed track suit, he looked the part. In fact, I can't think of any circumstances in which David would *not* look the part. Perhaps, I told myself ruefully, that was the benefit of a Cambridge education.

So Coach Dave was replaced by Coach David, and the team kept on winning. Win, after win, after dreary win. I wanted us to win just as much as ever, but now this was more from the fear of defeat than the anticipation of victory. Some of the wins meant more than others. Those over Manchester United and Birmingham meant that Kingston was now the only one team in the top division that we had never beaten. Generally, though, wins didn't mean as much as they used to.

If any reminder were needed that defeat was never far away, we crashed out of the National Cup to a Calderdale side gleefully led by none other than our former American star Micah, now arrived in Halifax via Plymouth. Americans never had much sense of geography. This was irritating for two reasons. It was our first ever game on national television, and it deprived me of the satisfaction of making a prompt call to whoever we were scheduled to play on the date of the semi-final, to confirm that we would like to postpone the game.

By the start of December we were 'joint top'; of the league, with eight wins from eight games. Even this was not the cause of excitement that it might have been. Kingston, the other joint leaders, were winning their games by an average of 20 or 30 points, we were typically winning by 10 or less. Portsmouth, who we were also yet to play, were only behind us because they had lost to Kingston.

So although our visit to Kingston was hyped as some sort of 'clash of the giants' by such as there was of the national basketball media, I approached it with trepidation. I was right. In common with the editorial policy, applied throughout this book, of thoroughly biased reporting, we will pass over what was widely touted as the biggest league match in our history. Suffice to say that we lost by 15. For those who want more detail, I add only that we never looked like winning.

By late January, our position in the league looked really weird. The defeat at Kingston had cruelly exposed any pretensions to challenge for the league, but hadn't diminished the ability to grind out wins against low and middle table teams, aided by our hopelessly lopsided fixture list. The returns against Kingston and Manchester United, and both games against Portsmouth, were all confined to the distant future. Five more completely unmemorable victories followed the Kingston game. By mid January we had the impressive but flattering record of 13 wins from 14 games.

Our next chance to challenge the big three was the visit to Portsmouth in late January, and was notable for three reasons – all bad. Fellow club Director Dave and I kicked off an evening of disasters by turning off the motorway without realising it, an apparently impossible feat for which thick fog was widely regarded as a pathetic excuse. Then the team weighed in by blowing a 15 point lead before finally losing by 10. Third, and worst of all, we were without Brian for most of the second half, and all of the next month, after an collision with some chairs that were far too close to the court. In fact, as the Portsmouth officials pointedly observed, they were almost as close as they were usually placed at Brunel.

*   *   *

One of the best known protest movements of the 1980s was the all-female camp protesting at the location of nuclear weapons on the Greenham Common air base. This did little to help the Government appreciate the dangers from nuclear weapons, but it did set them thinking about the danger from women. In future, it was decided that women should be properly occupied. There followed a campaign to break down all of those little barriers that prevented ordinary working class women from accessing the positions to which all respectable people aspired.

The agenda was typically eclectic, and very British. In February 1987, the Synod of the Church of England voted in favour of the ordination of women priests. In November, women were admitted to the Order of the Garter. The following year women were admitted to Magdalene College Cambridge for the first time. It was just one thing after another. And, if anyone doubted the wisdom of women seeking top positions, we had the experience of Margaret Thatcher to remind us of what happened when they reached them.

Carol's aspirations were more modest. In January 1987, however, she started a new job as a Lecturer at a further education college in Hounslow. This was not a ground breaking first for woman kind, but it was a turning point for the Kirkland household. We had both had jobs before, in the sense that we went out in the morning and a cheque arrived each month to thank us for doing so. But lecturing was not just a *job,* it was a *career.* It had a structure, it had a pension, it was respectable and it was something the people could understand in the pub.

I liked the idea of being married to a lecturer – even one who didn't know what she was supposed to be lecturing about. Formally, Carol had been appointed as a lecturer in business studies, with a particular brief for international trade, import and export studies. However, future international business moguls were short on the ground among the youth of Hounslow. There was a need for her to teach something else besides, but nobody seemed to know what. Maths was suggested at first, which sounded fine because at least she had an A level in the subject, but the numbers didn't add up there either. She ended up teaching Geography – a role not helped by her long standing vague belief that civilisation did not extend beyond Watford. Lessons were planned though urgent visits to the Brunel library on Saturday mornings, followed by furious scribbling on the team coach to away games. It would not surprise me if, to this day, there exists a generation of middle aged citizens of Hounslow who don't have the faintest idea which continent Berlin is on, but can cite every motorway service station between Uxbridge and Southampton.

*   *   *

If basketball and the 1980s had combined to teach me anything, it was the importance of money. I absorbed this lesson, perhaps to excess, but something concerned me. It was dawning on me that most of the people who owned clubs had secured their own fortunes, before deciding to squander large parts of them in basketball. I, by contrast, seemed intent on squandering my fortune before I had actually made it.

To remind me of this, Britain was on the verge of the most materialist general election of the twentieth century. History will judge that, by the early part of 1987, Britain was already losing its venture into casino capitalism, but no one yet realised this, and no one wanted to. With an irony that would not be recognised for several months, the Conservative manifesto proclaimed that 'for the first time in a generation, this country could look forward to an era of real prosperity and fulfilment'. Only one small corner of the document reminded us that 'money alone is not enough'. That, naturally, was the section that dealt with the funding of education.

By 1987 the materialist nature of British society was affecting all parties. Nowhere can this be seen more obviously than in the manifesto of the only party of the 1980s to retain its principles to the present day. Its manifesto reflected the materialist spirit of the age, including proposals to turn Britain into a giant theme park that would create eight million jobs, create a tax haven by re-routing the Channel Tunnel through Guernsey and, in a proposal which represented a particular threat to basketball, create a whole new industry by importing the American sport of dwarf throwing.

1987 was a watershed year for the Official Monster Raving Loony Party. At the time that we were preparing our final assault on Wembley, they were on the verge of winning their first ever seat on a local authority. If even they were becoming materialistic in their politics, I couldn't help but wonder whether I needed to review my aspirations, too.

*   *   *

Temporarily without Brian, and with the prospect of league honours diminishing, concentration wandered. If routine, uneventful wins were boring, then routine, uneventful defeats were even worse. We lost four out of the next six games after Portsmouth, briefly threatening our top four position. We stumbled over the finishing line into the play-offs, rather than crossing it with any conviction.

We held on to fourth place, although the difference between fourth and fifth didn't matter that much, because the two teams were seeded to play each other in the best of three play-offs. The fifth placed team was Leicester and, in view of recent form, the smart money was on them to cause an 'upset'. The lower team played at home first, and there were almost three thousand at Leicester's Granby Halls to cheer them on. We lost by three points, but only after a thrilling game that went to extra-time. Our form was returning, but at one-nil down in a three match series, our aim of getting to Wembley was hanging by a thread.

There was no place where that thread could have been more secure than the Brunel Sports Centre. My passion for basketball might have been waning over the previous few months, but the same could not be said for our home crowd. It was strange to think that two complete cohorts of students had passed through Brunel since the Ducks had embarked on their National League adventure, but during that period the noise and atmosphere had got ever more intense, while the numbers had got ever bigger. There was another packed house for the return game.

Whatever the reason, Leicester didn't have a prayer. We scored the first three baskets, and never looked back. After eight minutes, we led by 29–9; after 11, it was 39–11. With three minutes to go, the lead was a staggering 42 points, with the visitors in desperate foul trouble. The final margin was a 'mere' 30 points, but the style of the victory was probably as comprehensive as any that has ever taken place in the play-offs. We played everyone on our bench; eight registered on the score sheet; Leicester played just seven.

Being fourth, rather than fifth in the league gave us home advantage for the decider, too. I would have loved us to play this at Brunel, but that just wasn't possible. We had agreed months earlier that any decider would be at Crystal Palace, partly to help balance the merger, but also for a more fundamental reason. The middle two weeks of March were examination time at Brunel, and in the 1980s the Sports Centre was the only hall large enough to accommodate the annual exams. It was another reminder of our humble roots. The nice people from the badminton club would have been more than willing to accommodate us; the blank, anonymous faces from the Registry could not. The thought had regularly slipped my mind over the previous seven years, but Brunel was, first and foremost, a university. For universities examinations are, well, kind of important.

So Crystal Palace it had to be. It was the most famous venue in the entire league, twice the size of Brunel but nowhere near as full and with hardly any atmosphere. For a while, it looked as though things were going to be more difficult. Leicester again started slowly, and we soon led by 23-11, but they recovered composure and managed to lead by a single point at the interval. That, however, was the last time. A trio of baskets from Dale, followed by a trio from Mike Bett, followed by a couple from Brian re-established a double digit lead. The final score of 118-102 probably exaggerated the margin between the teams, but was definitely the right result. We were going to Wembley.

And that, for me, was the point at which the season belatedly clicked back into place. This was partly because the team had recovered its form with vengeance, partly because of the enthusiasm of everyone around me, and partly because even a cynic like me couldn't fail to be excited about having a team in the annual showpiece of basketball. There was another reason, too. By common consensus among the entire basketball community, we were now officially the underdogs again.

*   *   *

My direct contribution to the great event would, as for virtually every other game for the past seven years, be confined to the pre-match meeting and toss up. It was hardly onerous. As far as I knew, the Wembley court was not built on a slope, and I had every confidence that the post match refreshments would be up to scratch. None the less, I was determined to have a unique souvenir of what, I reasoned, would be a unique occasion. To obtain this, I returned to a long forgotten childhood hobby.

I had collected coins since the age of about 10. These were the pre-decimal days when it was possible to find rare dates in your change. I had lots of change because my dad used to manage a co-op store, and would lug bags and bags of it home on the bus for me to sort through. I made my first few pounds in life by carefully extracting 1953 pennies, 1952 sixpences and, on one memorable occasion, a 1930 half crown, from the cash takings of the Co-operative Wholesale Society (Hexthorpe Branch), and replacing them with shiny 1967 versions of my own. You see, now, what I mean when I say that I was never young.

I concluded that even a 1930 half crown (approximate value £3.50) would not suffice for my big nights at Wembley. Displaying a rare sense of style, I headed off to Lobell's coin shop in London, directly opposite the British Museum, and invested in the most expensive coin that I could afford. It was an attractive, but slightly worn – 14th-century groat. Six hundred years ago, a groat was worth four pence. In 1987, this one cost me £38.

Surprisingly, the English Basket Ball Association had overlooked the need to regulate the use of medieval coinage in pre-match meetings, so although my plea to both Commissioner and opposition promoter that we use the groat was met with mild surprise, no one could think of a reason to deny it. I even offered to let our opponents call on both occasions. My only condition was that I should catch the coin on its way down. My souvenir was over 600 years old. I wanted to take it home in one piece.

The groat did its job. Twice the opponents called heads, twice it came down tails. Whatever happened on court I, at least, would leave Wembley with a 100% success record. In the world of basketball, even this was not beyond suspicion. Fifteen minutes after the second toss up, the match Commissioner called me over and asked to see the coin again, inspecting it closely. He had, he admitted, no idea of how to distinguish between the two sides of the coin, and wanted me to assure him that it did, in fact, actually have a 'head'. After seven years, my reputation had hit an all-time low.

*   *   *

Having attended semi-final weekends as a supporter of Doncaster Panthers, I knew how quickly they could go flat. The first semi-final, between the first and fourth seeded teams, was played in the early evening of the Friday, before the stadium had filled up properly. For the losing team, the big weekend was effectively over virtually before it had started. The prospect of playing a third and fourth place game, on the early evening of the following day, and before an even emptier stadium, was little consolation.

All of which makes our 106-102 semi-final victory over Portsmouth, who had edged their way to the League Championship, all the more impressive. It was the second most important win in our history, and one which will go largely unreported here. This could, I suppose, be presented as a deliberate ploy, not to detract from the story of the following evening. The real reason is that I can't recall the details, and have no score sheet or press report to guide me. All that I do recall is that we led for most of the second half, that Paul Stimpson kept calm to score five vital points in the last minutes and that we, or at least some of the Brunel directors, became probably the first and only Wembley winners to celebrate with dinner at Pizza Hut. We were, undoubtedly, the most slobbish group of people ever to take a team to Wembley. We even ignored the slightly more up market Pizza Express across the road.

I for one considered the semi-final win as a means of extending the adventure of the weekend, rather than a significant step towards becoming national champions. Portsmouth may have topped the league, but Kingston, comfortable winners over Manchester United in the other semi-final, were the only team that we had never beaten, and it never occurred to me that this would be the occasion to do it.

The extent to which I was wrong about this added up to what Richard Taylor, in a two page special for *Basketball Monthly* that has been framed on the wall of our spare room for the last 20 years, termed 'one of Wembley's great stories'. 'On paper', the article gushed, 'they had little chance. Out on the floor the paper counted for nothing, especially if it was the colour of money. When it came to heart and the will to win, BCP London had millions to spend and plenty more on deposit in the bank'.

I wish I had a report from Richard of all of our games. It would have made this book so much easier for me to write, and you to read. He tells far more graphically than any score sheet could how Kingston scored the first five points, how we hit back with the next eight and how we never trailed again. Two minutes before half-time, the lead was an incredible 13 points, but then Kingston hit back with seven points of their own. It was 45–39 at the interval, and most people considered that Kingston would continue their fight back afterwards.

We all had a busy half-time. Coach David told *Basketball Monthly* how he had been furious at the lapse of concentration of the previous two minutes. 'I bawled them out', he recalls. 'At 13 points up we were a long way to having the game won. We'd given Kingston an awful lot to do. We let them back to six points down and that's nothing against any team, let alone Kingston'.

Fellow Director Dave and I spent the interval looking for a pint of beer. This should not have been too challenging, since the championships were being sponsored by Carlsberg and somewhere in our papers we both had tickets for the hospitality room. Official hospitality wasn't really our thing, though. Added to which we couldn't find our tickets or the room. On the other hand the public bars had huge queues and charged outrageous prices. In a rare show of extravagance, we bought a plastic glass full each and just managed to shepherd them back to our seats as the second half began.

The players had used their time more productively than we had. Instead of the expected Kingston surge, the teams traded baskets for a few minutes. After eight minutes, Kingston drew level at 66 all. It was widely assumed that this would be the turning point of the game. I will leave what happened next to my new found friend Richard Taylor:

'*In the moments while Kingston drew breath for their charge to the Championship, they lost the game and their title. Roberts scored off a rebound, Bett scored and drew a second foul off Bontrager, then made the bonus. Cadle called a time out and Lloyd immediately cut the lead to three. Politi scored, then drew an intentional foul off Bontrager, who was subbed, and scored the two frees. Davis took a rebound under his own basket, but Roberts ripped the ball from his grasp and went up to score. Barely three minutes after the last time out, Cadle was calling his second and last, with seven minutes still to play*'.

He goes on to tell how, in the dramatic final minutes, just about every loose ball seemed to end up in our hands, how the team successfully ran the clock down by keeping the ball for the maximum 30 seconds and how one such move, which ended after 28 seconds with Brian sinking a three pointer, proved the final clincher. Finally, he describes how 'baskets from Stimpson and Politi closed the account, scored between celebrations, hugging and hand slapping'. Richard, thankfully, was looking to the court for his literary inspiration. Had he looked at the Director's seats, he would have seen a very different picture – a combination of nerves, disbelief and stunned silence. So astonishing were the developments, that the pints of Carlsberg, procurement of which had taken so much of our time and money, lay forgotten and unnoticed at our feet.

When I read the article again, the nicest part is the way in which it recognises that the win was genuinely a combination of the strengths of the two clubs. From the Palace perspective, it describes how Paul, Mike and Coach David had 'kept alive the Palace traditions born during the club's record breaking success in the seventies and the eighties'. But it goes on to say how 'Dale Roberts, Brian Kellybrew, Julio Politi, Phil Ralfe and Cedrick Fredrick (and cagey club director John Kirkland) brought Brunel out of the second division just two years ago, and now they have a Wembley-winners medal'.

Well, actually they didn't. Or least, I didn't. I'm not sure how the goodies were divided up in the dressing room, but I was surprised to be presented afterwards with one of the 12 commemorative glasses given to the team by Carlsberg. There was also a rather big trophy, which looks as through it was made out of tin, which can still be found on a shelf in the Brunel Sports Centre. There was also a rather elegant piece of glassware, which naturally went to Crystal Palace.

If any proof were needed that our mergers had worked, it can be found in the final paragraphs of Richard's article. Julio's selection as man of the match was a source of particular pride, given the circumstances of his arrival two years earlier. Mike Bett, one of the recruits from Crystal Palace, was quoted as saying that this was the strongest team, physically and mentally, that he had ever played on. But the last comment fell to Dale – normally a man of few words. It was, he opined, down to which team had the most heart to win. 'And, man, we are all heart'.

*   *   *

The final hooter found me starting impassively at my still half empty pint of Carlsberg. Not finishing that drink was probably the most wasteful thing that I did in seven years as a basketball club director. I sometimes wonder if it is still there.

When athletes win gold medals at the Olympics, the first thing that television interviewers always ask them is 'how does it feel'? I always used to think that this was a profoundly stupid question. My own chances of winning an Olympic medal rank alongside those of my winning the Nobel Prize for literature –

roughly (on second thoughts precisely) zero. But if I ever did, I had assumed that I would feel absolutely ecstatic. And that is what I would tell every damn fool of a journalist who had the stupidity to ask such a damn fool question.

Being part of a club that took the national basketball championship at Wembley is the nearest that I will get to either experience, and my emotions were nowhere near as straightforward as I would have imagined. I guess that I had an underlying feeling of happiness and contentment, but perhaps this was so unusual that I didn't recognise it. The more immediate feeling that I remember was one of numbness, perhaps tempered with one of relief – a feeling that, after all the worries of basketball – not only in the past two hours, but the 2,500 or so days since Salih had almost run me over on the Brunel perimeter road, everything had turned out all right.

You will notice that I was starting to think of basketball in the past tense.

EPILOGUE

The Hollywood version of this story will end right here. The final scene could be our final basket dropping through the hoop at Wembley, possibly in agonising slow motion, followed by wild crowd celebrations. It could be the trophy being held up, probably by Phil, and being followed by the same crowd scenes. It could be me, staring blankly at my half empty pint of Carlsberg.

For an extra splash of meaning, the final scene could follow us back to the Brunel Sports Centre, where we did indeed return from Wembley for a night of celebration that lasted until dawn. This would take us neatly back to where our story began. A really clever Director would wind forward to the following Sunday, where amid scenes almost as tense as Wembley, our 'club' team, containing most of the players who started this story eight years previously, won the Middlesex Cup with a last second basket from Phil. Phil was the only member of the National League squad allowed to play for them, and only then because he had been a Middlesex League player first. It would show that the club had retained its roots, values and pure love for the game. A real tear jerker if ever there was one.

These endings assume that we all lived happily ever after. So we did, but not in the world of basketball. Whether within hours, days or weeks of that night at Wembley, many of us realised that this was the end of our adventure, and I doubt whether any of us regretted it since. 1987 was *so* the right time to leave basketball.

There were temptations. Being national champions, we were entitled to our place in Europe. It sounds ridiculous now, but who would have thought, just three years before, that Brunel would get the better of Manchester United, or take on and almost beat England? Perhaps the idea of Real Madrid, Inter Milan or Barcelona gracing the Brunel Sports Centre wasn't so crazy after all.

European Cup basketball, though, was not the same as Champions League football. There was no pot of gold, television or sponsorship rights, every chance that we would only get one home game and little prospect that we would be allowed to play it at Brunel. Worst of all, we had to get to the away venues. This club had difficulty getting to Derby and Worthing. Our one previous trip into Europe – the Sunday excursion to Rhonda – had left us staring over the edge of a mountain at one o'clock in the morning.

Then there was the problem of retaining a team to play in Europe. Brian, Dale and Julio were the envy of bigger and richer teams than ours, all the more so since they had proved their ability to work together as a unit. Of course, we would get some transfer fees, but these would be limited and nowhere near enough to find players of the same ability in the open market.

Added to all this was my growing recognition that I needed a career. I had dragged out the issue of whether university careers officers and electrical engineering departments were responsive to labour market needs for three years. The world could wait no longer for the answers. Nor would it pay me any longer to produce them. My contract was due to come to an end in September, and I needed a new job. The only position I knew that was compatible with running a basketball team was that of an academic, but in the Britain of the 1980s there were no tenured academic jobs left. Once again Margaret Thatcher had unwittingly come to my aid.

In any case, I no longer wanted to be an academic. I was tired of relatives asking every Christmas whether I was still at school. It was becoming hard to explain why, after another year of research, I could not explain within the attention span of an average auntie what I had 'discovered'. I was even having doubts myself. In 1981 and 1984 three year's job security had seemed like an eternity. By 1987, I was not so sure. I was now 29 years old, I had a wife and a mortgage. I was middle aged.

These were all good reasons for quitting on a high, but unknown to any of us there were even better ones. On 19 October 1987 the *Financial Times* index of leading shares lost £63 billion; by the end of the month, it had lost over 26% of its value. The impact was both financial and psychological. It marked the end of the Thatcherite boom, and the confidence that economic growth was a one way ticket. In the years that followed, millions of share holders, householders, company directors and their employees were to find out that it was not.

The effect on basketball was catastrophic. We were national champions for meanness. In fact we were obsessive about keeping our costs down, but even we had started to rely on the 'soft' sponsorship money that ultimately had its roots in economic confidence. No confidence, no sponsorship. We would not have been any exception to the trend.

Some showed more propensity to fight on. Crystal Palace had not recognised their limitations during the boom years, and certainly weren't going to start now. Their three Directors on our joint Board were keen to carry on at the Crystal Palace base and, after making sure that all debts and liabilities were covered, we wished them luck. They even secured some sponsorship for the coming season, but the costs were rising even faster. They finished the season in bottom place, left the league, briefly returned to in Division Two and made it again to the top division for two seasons in the mid-1990s, all without recapturing anything like the glory of their golden period. They were eventually merged into the London Towers, who themselves dropped out of the league. In doing so, Crystal Palace was seeking to protect a tradition more glamorous than any in British basketball. On the other hand, it was a long, lingering death. Some might disagree, but I never for a moment regretted the fact that Ducks quit when they did.

*　　*　　*

English basketball remains a total enigma. Months after we departed, the larger clubs got their way and established basketball's equivalent of the 'Premier League', It was administered independently from the EBBA, was 'British' rather then 'English' in order to accommodate (one) Scottish club and quickly dispensed with automatic promotion and relegation.

Abolishing promotion and relegation did not provide the stability that the leading clubs so eagerly sought. Of the 13 clubs who set out on the brave new world in 1987, only one remains in the same town today. Some drifted off quickly. Portsmouth lasted one more season. Calderdale backed out in 1989, unable to afford the court fees at their leisure centre. Solent was out by 1990. Ironically the one team to have survived in some form were Leicester – who later became based at, and sponsored by, a local university. Maybe the Brunel Ducks model, so widely ridiculed in the 1980s, was the right one after all.

Some of those who didn't go bankrupt merged, or sold their franchise. Perhaps the most grotesque example was Kingston. Deep in history, the Kingston franchise had started in Romford, before moving to Central London YMCA and then Kingston in 1979. After finishing second in the inaugural British Basketball League in 1988, Kingston sold their franchise to – Glasgow. Not too many supporters followed. They eventually returned to Guildford, eventually selling themselves again to London Leopards, and when they folded in 2002 a group of their supporters kept their name alive by merging with Ware Rebels – for whose pedigree see the saga of Hertfordshire basketball chronicled earlier in this book – and moving to Essex, where their predecessors had started out some 30 years and at least six venues previously. Even then the story did not have a happy ending, the newly merged team dropped out of the BBL a year later.

The British Basketball League has not delivered on other measures, either. Their entry on Wikipedia in 2010 stated bluntly that 'basketball receives little national media coverage'. The history of television deals – with MKTV, ITV Digital and Setanta – bears an uncanny resemblance to a directory of failed television companies. Even during its boom period of the 1990s, coverage of basketball on Sky did not approach the ratings or regularity achieved by Channel Four a decade earlier. The 1990s also saw progress on crowds – the record attendance for a BBL game of over 14,000 was set in 1995 – but this was a huge exception. Today several of the 13 member teams play on courts that barely meet the 1,000 capacity limit of the 1980s. Basketball remains a game of boom and bust.

This air of crisis came to a head in 2006, with the establishment by government, at the request of the basketball authorities themselves, of an independent panel to consider the entire structure of the sport. The review, conducted by a panel chaired by Tony Mallin, Chief Executive Officer of STAR capital partners, and former Vice-President of Hambros Bank, took place against a background of public fallouts between the English and British basketball leagues, declining attendances and international performance.

Its draft report, early the following year, reportedly concluded that current structures for administering the sport were completely unfit for purpose. The enquiry led, at various times, to Sport England suspending funding, the international governing body accusing the UK Government of seeking to take over the sport, and threatening to expel the country from international competition, and questions in the House of Commons. The final report concluded that basketball had huge potential that was not being fulfilled, but was dogged by too many competing interests. It was all *so* basketball, and *so* true. Whether or not the report surprised the basketball community of 2007 I'm not sure. It is very recognisable to someone who had been involved 20 years earlier.

*　　*　　*

Despite our efforts, Brunel University is flourishing. Six months after the victory at Wembley, and three days before the great stock market crash, the University found itself in the path of the fiercest gales to hit the south of England in decades. Much of the vegetation planted over the previous 20 years, disappeared at a stroke. It was seen as a setback in the transition from a grey, utilitarian campus of the 1960s to a modern, user friendly one.

In fact, the late 1980s were a watershed for Brunel in a more positive way. It had emerged from the financial pressures of the decade with its resources intact, and was ready to embark on a policy of expansion. It did this with enthusiasm – merging with other local colleges to boost numbers, utilising the economies of scale to full advantage, and finding ways to extract revenue from the huge bank of land which it now held. From the late 1990s, the revenue from this policy was spent in developing a range of facilities at which alumni of previous decades can only observe with awe. Brunel could not be described as unfashionable today.

Sport has been a major beneficiary of this expansion. The modest sports hall that we defended so vigorously as the home of the Brunel Ducks is still standing, but surrounded by a breathtaking range of facilities, including an indoor athletics track that was used as a training facility for the 2012 Olympics, and a purpose built basketball and netball facility. The university has produced a string of international medallists and won national titles, indeed one of the mergers was with the West London Institute of Education, which also produced several Ducks players.

I sometimes wonder where the Ducks could have got to with the facilities, personnel and resources that the University has today. But I'm not complaining. One way or another, the University put more into the Ducks than anyone could have hoped for given the financial situation of the 1980s – more than could ever have been shown on any balance sheet, and almost certainly more than it itself realised. We certainly owe Brunel, rather than the other way round. I hope that this book will start to repay the debt.

*   *   *

Carol and I survived without basketball, too. It was amazing how many other things we found to do. Carol moved on from a career in importing, to one which embraced teaching others how to import, organising other teachers and eventually managing college finances so that they could teach more for less. To the astonishment of my supervisor, and amidst widespread apathy in the academic community, I completed my doctorate, thus increasing the completion rate of 1981 Brunel politics PhD starters from 0% to 100% at a stroke. I promptly moved from being an academic, to administering academics, encouraging academics to be even more productive academics and developing the next generation of academics. A combined total of over 50 years happy and reasonably well rewarded effort, without actually producing anything. Margaret Thatcher would think it scant reward for all her support.

To make absolutely sure that we couldn't change our minds, we stared a family. Less than two years after our great night at Wembley, Christopher arrived. Three years later, he was joined by Stephen. Suddenly I realised why so many basketball players, coaches and directors were single, or at least childless. Running a basketball team had plenty of similarities with having a house full of kids, but doing the two at the same time would have been impossible.

In the 25 years since our night at Wembley, I have seen two top level basketball matches. The first was at the end of 1987, when Carol and I went to a game at Crystal Palace with the sole aim of getting our final cheque to the VAT authorities signed. We didn't even stay to the end. It just didn't seem that interesting any more.

The second game was several years later. We were staying with my parents for Easter, when I noticed that Doncaster, briefly reincarnated and in the top division, were playing host to Birmingham, and suggested to Christopher – now eight years old – that we might go. Carol looked horrified, and with good reason. The previous year I had lured him to his first football match at Rotherham, with the promise of a Mars bar every time they scored. It had been an expensive decision in more ways than one. Rotherham, third from bottom of the league and without a win for over a month, inexplicably scored three goals in 10 minutes, and went on to win 5-1. Worse even than the cost of the Mars bars, Christopher was hooked. It was an affliction from which he has never recovered.

As a way of keeping a lid on our enthusiasm, Carol decided to take Stephen swimming at the same venue, to keep a close eye on things. She needn't have worried. Doncaster were the underdogs, they made a brave fist of it before losing, and for a few minutes we got quite enthusiastic. As things turned out, though, we were watching their last ever game. Doncaster went out of business. It wasn't the first time that they had dropped out of the top division, but it was the last. So the game didn't reignite my enthusiasm for basketball, but it did bring my basketball watching career round to a neat full circle. It was watching Doncaster bravely lose that had first provoked my interest, some 20 years previously.

Christopher and Stephen can point to many flaws in their upbringing. An obsession with basketball will not be one of them. As their childhood progressed, basketball affected them in only one material way. They came to learn that – however urgent the need to record a television programme, there were two dusty videos at the back of the cupboard that should not be used on any account. One is our wedding video, the other some of the last remaining footage of the Brunel Ducks in action – a home win against Bracknell in 1986.

Apart from being produced by the same person, in the same year, the videos have two things in common. We never watch either of them, and we never, ever, want to wipe them. I hope that we never will.

Printed in Great Britain
by Amazon

42209536R00111